ANNE ORTLUND

DISCIPLINES
OF THE
HEART
Tuning
Your Inner Life
to God

ANNE ORTLUND

DISCIPLINES
OF THE
HEART
Tuning
Your Inner Life
to God

WORD BOOKS
PUBLISHER
WACO, TEXAS

A DIVISION OF
WORD, INCORPORATED

DISCIPLINES OF THE HEART

Unless otherwise indicated, Scripture quotations are from The New International Version of the Bible, copyright © 1978 by the New York International Bible Society. Used by permission of Zondervan Bible Publishers.

Other Scripture quotations are from the following sources:

The King James Version of the Bible (KJV).
The New American Standard Bible (NASB), © The Lockman Foundation 1960, 1962, 1963, 1968, 1971, 1972, 1973, 1975, 1977.
The New Testament in Modern English (PHILLIPS) by J. B. Phillips, published by the Macmillan Company, © 1958 by J. B. Phillips.

Emphasis in Scripture quotations (italics) is the author's.

Library of Congress Cataloging in Publication Data:

Ortlund, Anne.
    Disciplines of the heart.

    1. Women—Religious life. I. Title.
BV4527.078   1987   248.8'43   87-8236
ISBN 0-8499-0565-6

Printed in the United States of America

This edition has been produced for members of Family Bookshelf and is reprinted by arrangement with Word Books, Waco, Texas.

To my granddaughters, tomorrow's beautiful women:

Mindy Harrah   Lisa McClure
Beth Anne Harrah   Laurie McClure
Krista Ortlund

Contents

Foreword

Bookwriting isn't easy.

You write and write and write, and the thing eventually begins to take shape and form and to harden more and more into its own personality. Before you know it, it has a will of its own and has risen up and is looking you straight in the eye and telling you what to do.

"Chapters 3 and 4 need a little lightening," I said, "a bit of humor, a personal anecdote or two. . . ."

"No, they don't." The book had firmly removed the pen from my hand. "Quit fiddling. Don't you change me. Don't you touch me."

Timidly I withdrew. "I was just trying to help," I offered uncertainly. "My other books had more light touches. . . ."

"I'm not your other books," was his reply. "I am the way I am, and that's the way I'm supposed to be."

"But people might have trouble wading through chapters 3 and 4; they might quit reading and miss the important part," I said, struggling to match his authority.

"That's their problem," he answered, and he seemed to have grown until now he was towering above me.

I searched his face—the face I knew so well, line for line. And I dared to like him. In fact, I truly admired him. I have to say it—he's better than me. He has more wisdom than I have; he is *more than me*—far more.

I relaxed.

"You win," I whispered.

ANNE ORTLUND

DISCIPLINES
OF THE
HEART
Tuning
Your Inner Life
to God

Chapter 1

You're at a crossroads.

1

There you are—a woman.

How is life for you?

Have you too much to do?

Are you loved?

Are you overspending?

Are you gripped by a habit—and worried?

Are you young but unattractive? Beautiful but aging? Losing your health? Wealthy? Shy?

Are you surrounded by clamoring kids? Oppressed by your boss at work? Popular on your campus?

Are you satisfied?

Are you married to a loser? Unusually gifted? Single and fulfilled?

Are you embarrassed over whatever you're like?

There are so many kinds and conditions of women in this world, millions and millions of them—some hurting, some happy . . . some pushers and shovers, others the pushed and the shoved. . . .

But out of them all, only you are you. And here you are, in this special moment, starting to read my book.

This one is a sequel to an earlier book, *Disciplines of the Beautiful Woman,*[1] and I'm praying that through it God will give you individual, personal renewal from your toes up—a renewal as thorough as the one He gave me a few years ago, the one that for me began all this bookwriting!

Disciplines of the Beautiful Woman was the easiest to write of all my books. It speaks of living your external life for God: using a notebook, keeping a desk, organizing yourself and your home. . . . It gives you a hands-on examination

---

1. Anne Ortlund, *Disciplines of the Beautiful Woman* (Waco, TX: Word, 1977).

12

of Western-culture, middle-class, female Christian living. It's even read by a lot of men, too, because it has to do with being well managed and goal oriented and productive, and we all want that. I'm glad God let me write it.

But I long that the name *Anne Ortlund* be associated with more than notebooks and closets. For tools to help us live in Christ are only tools.

I can have the latest electric toothbrush and the best toothpaste—and still not brush my teeth.

I can have the most expensive stationery and the finest pen and a supply of stamps—and still not write that letter I need to write.

I can have a wonderfully equipped kitchen and plenty of food—and still not put a meal together. (Don't pursue me on that one.)

Tools are only tools.

I'm painfully aware that I can have my Bible and notebook as close as my elbow—and still snap at my husband, Ray, when my heart's out of tune with God.

You probably know what I mean. The exterior is easier than the interior, isn't it?

The rich young ruler of Mark 10 knew that, too. He said he'd done what he could—but he still had a deep itch inside of him that wasn't satisfied yet. So he came to Jesus—and "Jesus looked at him *and loved him.*"

And, oh, the Lord looks at you right now and loves you! He loves your external efforts in His direction; He isn't despising you. Parents love their children's beginning efforts, and God feels tenderly about every external "upward motion" you make.

But how's your interior? Are you discouraged over your progress? Are you feeling you should have gotten farther along than you have?

Or maybe you're just plain becoming disillusioned. You're suspecting the Christian life is overadvertised; you haven't achieved all this peace and power and joy that you hear talked about so glibly. You haven't experienced much victory over the "old nature" still within you. Your circumstances still tend to worry you or depress you, and when you feel you need God the most, He often seems the farthest away.

Well, you don't want to go back to the old life—but surely you missed a turn in the road somewhere! It should have been better than this. . . . Is that how you feel?

So, God is prodding me.

Writing a book on the external life was a start, but the need is deeper. At women's conferences I sense the Christian woman's hunger for God, her hunger to grow, her hunger for solutions to her problems—her longing to *make it* in life, to be looked on as a contemporary "beautiful woman" filled with true godliness and grace.

Interesting as I remember the timing of the writing of *Disciplines of the Beautiful Woman*. . . . One publisher said women weren't interested in getting organized and turned the manuscript down. And when the good people at Word Books accepted it, still some of them wondered if that word *disciplines* in the title wouldn't turn women off and limit sales. But the time for the book was right, and God's women were helped and are still being helped.

I'm convinced that *now the time is right for a book on the "inside job."*

It's later in the world.

Sin is greater now.

The dangers are greater.

The pain is greater.

And your desire for internal answers is stronger.

I believe you will read today more boldly, more deeply, more seriously, perhaps more desperately. You're hungry for more than being organized and productive; you're hungry for a deep heart life of holiness and happiness and serenity.

I believe it's God's time for this book—and I believe *it's your time.*

This one may not duplicate the truths you currently know. It may even ruffle your feathers a bit. So be it.

A famous evangelist's preaching once prompted a critic to say, "Don't you know you're rubbing the cat's fur the wrong way?"

"Then," said the evangelist, "let the cat turn around."

14

Turn your mind around.

2

Your whole life—like mine, my friend—is determined by what happens between your ears. That's why the message of this book on a woman's heart life, thought life, between-the-ears life, is so crucially important.

In fact, between your very two ears right now you may be thinking, "This book is starting out a little serious and heavy; I think I'll quit and get a decorating magazine. After all, I only have so much time to relax. . . ." But I'm praying the Holy Spirit will keep tugging at you; you could be at the crossroads of your life and not know it. *(Lord, keep this reader reading, and open up her heart to You.)*

You know about Gallup Polls. Dr. George Gallup, Sr., was a Christian, and one of his last polls before his recent death was designed to probe more deeply into the spiritual condition of his fellow Americans. The poll led him to two conclusions:

1. That religious fervor in America is at an all-time high, and
2. That religious *knowledge* in America is at an all-time low. (That is, fewer know where to find the accounts of the life of Jesus or the Ten Commandments in the Bible, and so forth.)

Dr. Gallup's projection as a result of this poll was that in the years immediately ahead America will go one of two ways. Either:

1. We will experience the greatest spiritual revival we have ever known, or
2. We will see our greatest degeneration into cults and false religions.

I believe the choice will depend on whether American Christians *discipline their hearts*, whether they go deeper internally, whether they deliberately seek for and get settled in God and His Word—or whether they don't.

We're still hanging in the balance.

Religious fervor doesn't seem to have slackened. Ray and I, holding conferences on spiritual renewal all over the world, stay solidly booked several years in advance. And everywhere we go, we're touched at how earnest and tender-hearted God's people are.

It may not be too late. But certainly the direction our country takes depends in part on whether preachers and writers will take the hunger seriously enough and feed people not chaff, but God's truth!

On the other hand, many who aren't grounded in this biblical knowledge are already flocking to new TV shows, new places, new experiences where they're "freed," "made aware," "released," "fulfilled"—sensations on which their "self" dotes, and which appeal to this feelings-oriented age.

"Ray," I asked a while back, "if you were to write a book for a Christian woman about her heart, what would you say?"

"I'd tell her about her great personal need to learn to think biblically," said Ray. "I'd write a book that was a big dose of *truth,* and I'd seek to convince her that the source of truth is the Word of God."

He'd just put into my hands a book called *The Christian Mind,* which has in it this punchy British comment on truth:

> If schoolboy "X" has got the right answer to a sum, and his eleven companions have got various wrong answers, then "X" would be a fool to compromise by accepting a figure averaged out from the twelve exercise books.
>
> Christian truth is objective, four-square, unshakable. . . .
>
> [Truth is like] a lighthouse lashed by the elemental fury of undisciplined error. Those who have come to reside in the truth must stay there. . . . Truth is most certainly a shelter.[1]

---

1. Harry Blamires, *The Christian Mind* (Ann Arbor, MI: Servant Books, 1978), 113–114.

Women by the millions today (men, too) are unsheltered, untaught, unfed, and tossing around on stormy, dangerous waves. They're exposed to every opinion and fad, right and wrong. And they're prime candidates to end up on the rocks of satanic religions.

I want this book, then, to be two things:

1. To be rooted in the Bible—to fight against biblical ignorance before it's too late; and
2. To be practical—because your great need is also concrete, measurable obedience to what you learn.

I want to affect you deeply—not just to influence you to start living out of a notebook or cleaning out your closets, but to affect you in your heart, between your ears, in the way you think—where your true living either wins or loses.

I hope you'll have both Bible and notebook in hand as you read this book, and that you'll not only *read* but *do*. Read these first five chapters to get a running start, but after that there will be guidelines for you to follow for on-the-spot obedience. I want the reading of this book to be not only a true event for you, but the beginning of new processes in your life, new "holy habits." Maybe you'll gather a little group of friends and experience it and study it together, holding each other accountable for taking new steps of obedience. Buy yourselves each a notebook to be ready to "do the truth."[2]

And, oh, I want this book to guide you through the Scriptures, so that you see God's reason for reaching for you in the first place and see His grand purposes—with you yourself in mind—behind His Cross: to make you holy as He is holy, and happier than you ever dreamed. I want you to be able to say with no qualifications, as He wants you to say, "Surely goodness and mercy shall follow me all the days of my life!"

---

2. If you want to buy "Disciplines Notebooks" from me, write for order forms to Anne Ortlund, Renewal Ministries, 4500 Campus Drive, Suite 662, Newport Beach, CA 92625, U.S.A.

3

What kind of realistic, nitty-gritty, earthly life does God have in mind for a woman He creates—a woman, for instance, like you?

God wants you to be truly good and truly happy.

Does your heart agree? Does something inside you say that it must be true, that it makes sense, that He didn't go to all that trouble to create you and save you to have you turn out otherwise?

And yet if your Christian life so far doesn't seem particularly good or happy, what do you do? Scale down your expectations?

Maybe you've decided that heaven will come later and your earthly life is still supposed to be full of hassle—but at least it's more bearable than if you weren't a Christian. You've concluded that nobody's perfect yet and that you'll still sin quite a bit, but at least not as much as a non-Christian—and anyway, you're forgiven.

If on a scale of one to ten your expectations are between five and seven, you've got plenty of company. Typical Christians don't really dare to expect too much. Their lives are full of heat and dust and friction, and they've rejected as unrealistic the possibility of being too terrific.

What about you?

Maybe you're a business woman and you certainly love the Lord, but after all, God only made one Mother Theresa. . . . Or you're a homemaker who serves in your church, but you've decided you were never meant to be some sort of Jesus freak. Maybe you've even deluded yourself into thinking your Christian life is "normal" when in fact it's simply stale, commonplace, timid, and ineffective.

For many Christian women life is grey—neither awful nor wonderful.

Their rationale is: if the truly wonderful isn't realistically possible in this life, why expect it and be disappointed? Or if it doesn't seem to be popular, why stick out like a sore thumb?

So in the whole Christian world there's lots of compromise, lots of lethargy, lots of conformity to the mediocre, lots of tolerance of sin and therefore lots of sin. And because of sin, there's lots of pain—you can be sure God sees to that.

With an eased-up view of sin, the heavy emphasis is on grace and forgiveness so that the idea becomes "God forgives us; let's forgive each other. Then we can do anything and still accept each other." Romans 6:1 is shocked at this kind of attitude: "Shall we sin to our heart's content and see how far we can exploit the grace of God?" (PHILLIPS).

The Bible smashes that kind of thinking. God overturns it all like overturning money tables in the temple. May this book strongly say to you, "THUS SAYS THE LORD"—not "Thus says the majority"! Reader, like a little child, hear His Word freshly and turn your mind around.

God didn't plan for your Christian life to be grey. No, no, no!

Take the book of Proverbs, for instance. Proverbs doesn't say that your life should be somewhere between awful and wonderful. Proverbs says the fool's life is awful and the believer's life is *wonderful!*

Period!

People weak in the Bible are uncomfortable with such black-and-white pronouncements. They "think grey"—so they live grey, have grey friends, sin a little or a lot, and hurt a little or a lot. And probably they're bored, bored, bored.

Proverbs, however, says black is BLACK:

The way of the wicked is like deep darkness; they do not know what makes them stumble (4:19).

[They] lie in wait for their own blood (1:18).

20

[The house of the adulteress] leads down to death. . . .
None who go to her return (2:16–19).

Satan tries to make the wicked look . . . well, shades of
grey somewhere between soft dove and sophisticated charcoal. The "scoundrel and villain" of Proverbs 6:12–15 we're
supposed to half admire; he seems bad, steely cool, and
kinda cute—like the hero of some TV or movie detective
plot. He's the one who

> goes about with a corrupt mouth,
> who winks with his eye,
> signals with his feet
> and motions with his fingers,
> who plots evil with deceit in his heart—
> he always stirs up dissension.

But God's future for him is death:

> Therefore disaster will overtake him in an instant;
> he will suddenly be destroyed—without remedy.

The life of the fool, says Proverbs, isn't even a pretty
lacquer black—it's ugly and dirty: "The name of the wicked
will rot" (10:7)!

On the other hand, dear lady, if you love God, take a
look at *what He says your life is to be like*, reasonably and
realistically:

> [You] will live in safety
> and be at ease, without fear of harm (1:33).

> When you lie down, you will not be afraid; . . .
> your sleep will be sweet.
> [You will] have no fear of sudden disaster
> or of the ruin that overtakes the wicked,
> for the Lord will be your confidence
> and will keep your foot from being snared (3:24–26).

No shades of grey here! Blessings will crown your head
(10:6). You'll point the way of life to others (10:17). You'll be

granted what you desire (10:24). You'll stand firm forever (10:25)—you'll never be uprooted (10:30). You'll win favor and a good name in the sight of God and man (3:4) . . . and on and on.

Does God lie, or does He even exaggerate? Then do you dare think this is all too good to be true?

The grey Christian woman tends not to take God really seriously. Even her "believing" is grey, so she gets a life about the same shade.

What about you?

Will you read another chapter and lift your eyes to the possibility that your life could really be *wonderful?*

Chapter 4

---

*Dare to believe
your life could be wonderful.*

4

If you haven't before, deep inside your heart begin to believe a daring truth: God doesn't want you to live a mediocre life. In fact, here's His flat-out goal for you:

That you may become blameless and pure, children of God without fault in a crooked and depraved generation, in which you shine like stars in the universe (Phil. 2:15).

That you may be able to discern what is best and may be pure and blameless until the day of Christ, filled with the fruit of righteousness (Phil. 1:10–11).

You don't have to "live grey," feeling dirty, unworthy, mediocre, unfulfilled, and guilty.
And, my friend, whatever God asks you to be, He enables you to be! Second Peter 1:3 says that His divine power has given you *everything you need* for life and godliness! He says that you may even "participate in the divine nature and escape the corruption in the world caused by evil desires" (2 Pet. 1:4).

"How can such a thing be?" we ask in wonder, the way the Virgin Mary asked of the Christmas angel. And back from Colossians 2:9 comes the lofty magnificence of this bold statement of truth:

In Christ all the fullness of the deity lives in bodily form, and you have been given fullness in Christ!

Then how could you or I insult Him by living a cheap, grey, inconsequential life? He has promised that "He will be the sure foundation for your times, a rich store of salvation and wisdom and knowledge" (Isa. 33:6)!

And how does the power for this come to you?

Ray was walking one day on the beach near our Southern California home, thinking about the power of God in our lives.

Just then he happened to come upon a dead sea gull washed up on the shore. He thought, "If I threw the carcass of this gull up into the air, gravity would make it fall to the ground with a thud. On the other hand, over my head sea gulls are flying everywhere."

What was the difference? It was life. The power of gravity was just as great on the living gulls as on the dead ones, but the greater power of life within lifted the living ones and overcame gravity's downward drag.

So Romans 8:9-11 says,

> You . . . are controlled not by the sinful nature but by the Spirit, if the Spirit of God lives in you. . . . And if the Spirit of him who raised Jesus from the dead is living in you, he who raised Christ from the dead will also give life [that lifting, overcoming life-force] to your mortal bodies.

God's resurrection power is the greatest upward force of all forces; that's the power for godliness that He's put within your very own body.

And the Apostle Paul prays that you will *understand this power*, dear person feeling downward pulls in your life! So few do understand—and understanding makes all the difference, as you'll see in the next chapter.

He prays "that the eyes of your heart may be enlightened" (would you ask God to open the eyes of your heart?)—

> that you may know . . . his incomparably great power for us who believe. That power is like the working of his mighty strength, which he exerted in Christ when he raised him from the dead (Eph. 1:18-20).

Talk about getting a drink from a fire hydrant. . . .

When you take this seriously, you want to ask, "Lord, is that an economical use of power? Was there some reason You really needed to take the most gigantic upward force in the entire universe and put it inside lil' ol' me?"

Picture J. Paul Getty drawing from his vast financial resources a coin to make a phone call. Then maybe you can begin to understand that you have absolutely unlimited power for godly living, and that when you draw on it every minute from here to eternity, the amount you'll use will be laughably, ridiculously small compared with the amount that's left still available for you.

Chapters 5, 6, and 7

Learn to let God work in you.

5

Then why do so many Christians live grey, struggling, carnal lives? Because they haven't comprehended the vastness of the power within them and what to do with it.

"Well, what *are* we to do with it?" you're asking.

And I answer, "Nothing."

"What?" you squawk. "That's crazy. Of course we're to do something. We have to do something to take advantage of all that power."

A woodpecker was once pecking away on a great tree. Suddenly a huge bolt of lightning struck the tree and with enormous noise and force split it right down the middle, straight to its very roots.

The poor little woodpecker found himself on the ground nearby, half-dead, his feathers torn and singed. And when he gathered himself together he croaked, "I didn't know I could do it!"

So God desires to show His great power in our lives, and we croak, "Now, what shall I do? I certainly have to do something to make this happen."

The answer is really "Stand back!" It's "Take God seriously! Accept His enormous power in your life; believe it, and be ready for miracles!"

"What must I do," asked the Philippian jailer, "to be saved?"

And Paul answered, "Believe. Just believe, and you'll be saved—that's all it takes. Don't 'do'; you'll just get in the way. Let God do the 'doing'!"

And that night, as the jailer simply "[came] to believe in God" (Acts 16:34), the Lord God Almighty mysteriously reached down out of eternity and chose him, applied the eternal work of the Cross to that man's account, wrote his name in the Lamb's book of life, washed him of his sins, caused him to be born into His heavenly family, breathed into him eternal life, removed all condemnation from him, deposited in him His Holy Spirit as a "down payment" of more to come, bestowed on him all the riches of His grace, eternally predestined him to be conformed to the image of His Son, made him a co-heir with Christ of all things, called him, justified him, sanctified him, glorified him—and so much more that it will take all eternity for that jailer to discover what God "did" the instant he believed!

When we're itchy to "do," it's usually because we really *don't believe*, so we're trying to help God out. In Jesus' hometown, "he did not do many miracles because of their lack of faith" (Matt. 13:58). They didn't take seriously His supernatural power so available for them, so He didn't use it! And when we don't understand His resurrection power within us, we develop an activist religion that crowds out the possibility of that giant, explosive power's working in our lives.

Now, the confusion comes because we don't see clearly that there are two sides in Christianity: His side and our side, His dazzling white and our black. (Face it: in ourselves, in our own strength, we're black.) Most Christians mix the two—some of God in their lives, some of themselves, some white, some black—and come out grey.

But God wants to take over completely and use His power to make you, my friend, as dazzling white as Himself!

> Just as he who called you is holy, so be holy in all you do; for it is written: "Be holy, because I am holy" (1 Pet. 1:15–16, Lev. 11:44–45).

> "It is God's will that you should be holy" (1 Thess. 4:3).

Now, if you're objecting, "But I can't; that's impossible," you're absolutely right. Whew, you see it! That's so important. If you thought you could, you'd be another woodpecker.

You can't be holy. You can't be truly good. You can't, in

yourself, be "pure and blameless" and all those things God seems to be insisting you must be.

Take a look at the two sides of this thing.

Ray and I have a big porcelain conch shell in our kitchen, and sometimes I fill it with fruit. I had a gorgeous peach in it recently, a soft gold with a perfect rosy blush on it. At just the right moment I carried it to the sink, leaned over, and took a big bite. Yuk! I hadn't noticed the other side; it was black with rot and mold. That peach had two sides.

When I saw only one side of my peach I described it as perfect. Someone seeing the other side would say, "No, that peach is rotten."

Now, there are two distinct sides in Christian righteousness, and they are totally different and must not be confused.

God's part is to work —with all that divine, all-encompassing power.

Our part is to trust Him to do it.

A century ago Christians knew this truth well. But we forgot it, and our egos took over, and we became such busy little woodpeckers that our heads hurt! Then we got stressed out, so we've given up and settled for less.

Certainly there's plenty of work to be done. We are trapped in bad habits and self-centeredness and temper and all that opposes God. Those things are the *fruit* of sin—that we worry about and try to keep somewhat under control, or at least under cover.

But the real problem is even more serious. It's the *root* of sin—that consistent, basic tendency to sin which made Paul cry out, "What a wretched man I am! Who will rescue me from this body of death?" (Rom. 7:24).

You can't rescue yourself.

> Were the seas water
> And all the land soap,
> If Thy blood not wash me,
> There is no hope.[1]

---

1. John Donne (1573–1631).

So God does the work! He steps in and rolls up His sleeve and bares His·mighty arm, and does it all.

Oh, my friend! If you could understand what He's done for you—and what He's doing—and what He will yet do—!

As Isaiah 63:1–10 explains it, Jesus Christ our Lord,

Dismayed over the death-sins in which we're totally—and willingly—enmeshed,

Feeling intensely the loneliness and rejection of being the only One who cares enough to do something about it,

Dons His soldier's garb and takes sword in hand and comes down to do what He knows, for love's sake, He must do.

He battles us sinners to the death—His death—becoming totally bloody and ruined and eternally stained and scarred—

For what?

To rescue the very ones He's battling—to rescue us, His enemies, whom He loves so passionately—to rescue the ones who fight Him, bloody Him, hurt Him, defeat Him, wound and kill Him,

To rescue us so that He can rise, scarred and bloodied, to enfold us tenderly to His breast and gently clear our vision so we can see how deeply He loves us, and then to spend eternity pouring out His kindness upon the precious ones He's rescued, comforting us and sustaining us and doing uncounted good things for us all the days of our eternal lives.

Alleluia!

So, there are two sides. His part is to do it all. And our part is to let Him do it—and hopefully to thank Him and praise Him and marvel over it all!

But when we speak of resting and trusting, it's not as though nothing were happening. Everything is happening! He is thrilled over you, the one He's restored to Himself, and He is constantly, powerfully working on your behalf.

There was a time when God rested: on the seventh day of creation, when He had finished all His creating work (Gen. 2:2). But then Adam and Eve and all the rest of us sinned, and God hasn't rested since. Jesus said, "My Father is always at his work to this very day, and I, too, am working" (John 5:17). And God won't rest again until you are totally redeemed, and until all sin and death and everything that hurts you is completely destroyed (1 Cor. 15:24–28). He loves you so much!

But does it gall you to think of just letting Him do everything?

Between your two ears, my friend, your successful living depends on your seeing the difference between these two sides. Unless you understand the mighty, eternal, efficient, sufficient work of God for you, you'll try to lend a hand and you'll mess up your life.

A few decades ago, when we forgot the ancient, biblical truth of God's work and our rest (our theological roots), then certain hymns fell out of favor. Hymns that emphasized our part of trusting Him sounded as if Christianity had had the juice turned off, as if it was no go, as if it was dead in the water.

With all there is to *do* in the Christian life, why would we sing songs like this—

> Jesus, I am resting, resting
> In the joy of what Thou art;
> I am finding out the greatness
> Of Thy loving heart?

Forget this resting stuff; let's get busy! Let's GOFORIT!

Jean Sophie Pigott wrote that wonderful hymn I just quoted in 1876, just one year after Bradford Torrey wrote this next one. It's even quieter, so it died even sooner.

Right now, do something interesting: read this hymn as an activist, roll-up-your-sleeves-and-hit-that-target modern Christian, and see how it will turn you off. Then read it a second time in the light of the full-orbed, unceasing, supportive, caring energies of God on your behalf, and see how it will turn you on.

Here's the hymn:

> Not so in haste, my heart!
> Have faith in God and wait.

Although He linger long,
He never comes too late.
  He never comes too late;
  He knoweth what is best.
  Vex not thyself in vain;
  Until He cometh, rest.
Until He cometh, rest,
Nor grudge the hours that roll;
The feet that wait for God
Are soonest at the goal,
  Are soonest at the goal
  That is not gained by speed;
  Then hold thee still, my heart,
  For I shall wait His lead!

Are you feeling tense these days? Are you overworked, stressed out? Keep reading! Do yourself a favor and keep reading.

I spoke recently to the Fellowship of Christian Airline Personnel in Dallas. (What a wonderful bunch they are!) I asked Pam, a pretty flight attendant, for illustrations on what it means to trust in God and let Him work.

Pam was great! First she told me how hard it is to diaper her one-year-old.

"You never saw such a squirmer," she said. "If she would just relax and let me be in control, I could put on her diaper in half the time, and then she could go have fun again." (Christian, think about it.)

Then she told me about her sister's little boy's getting his first haircut. That barber had to be quick! Just as he'd be ready to snip, Jason would wiggle, turn his head, or get bored and want out of the chair. Many rubber-duck-squeaks later, the job was finally done, but that was getting a haircut the hard way. Jason had trouble being quiet to let the barber do his work.

I told Pam about how my fair skin doesn't like California sun, so now and then I have to have the dermatologist remove sun damage. This last time it was everything on my face at once. You better believe I lay absolutely quiet on that operating table while the doctor froze, cut, and burned.

Listen, when it comes to getting the power to live a holy, happy life—let's you and me admit it's not our strong suit. Let's stay quiet and let Almighty God do for us everything we need done. "Be still before the Lord," says Psalm 37:

> Commit your way to [Him];
>   trust in him and he will do this:
> He will make your righteousness shine like the dawn.

Now Work into Your Life
What You've Been Reading.

If the message of this book from God's Word is going to be life-changing for you, you must insist on a dead boulevard stop at this point.

Don't race on to the next chapter.

Tell God you have this tendency to St. Vitus' Dance—to nervous rushing which keeps you living on the surface instead of going underneath!

"Current Christianity," said someone, "is seventy-three miles wide and half an inch deep." Will you personally help to reverse that trend?

Within the next twenty-four hours, before you go on to chapter six, take a full thirty minutes to reread this fifth chapter. Then, just *sit before the Lord.*

"Be still," as Psalm 37:7 commands, and during that time write in your notebook a prayer to Him.

Surrender your heart to Him, telling Him you want to turn a new corner in your Christian life.

Surrender your mind to Him. Tell Him you want to learn to think well, to think biblically, to walk in truth, to be established and settled in His doctrine.

If you are several in a group, end your meeting now with a time of silence. Afterward, if the Spirit leads, humbly pray together about your new determination. Then make the thirty-minute experience your "homework" before meeting again.

6

I haven't told many stories and entertained you much so far, have I? That's because, as I said, I believe you're ready to read more boldly, more deeply, more seriously. Here's a truth for you that could truly establish and strengthen and settle you in God:

God is at work in everything.

Do you believe that? You won't truly rest and trust if you believe He's only at work in some areas of your life, and the rest is up to you. Then you'll come out grey! And hassled. And tired.

Grey Christians think God is at work in some activities but not in others. Sometimes I've heard Christians pray when they come to a church meeting or a retreat, "Lord, it's so good to come back to You out of the bustle and stress. . . ." I want to interrupt, "He's been with you all the time! How tragic if you've been living until now as if you were on your own!"

Grey Christians think God is at work on Sundays but not from Monday to Saturday. They come to church with their empty buckets, in a sense saying, "Fill 'er up, preacher! It's got to last me another whole week!" They don't know that Jesus said, "Whoever believes in me . . . streams of living water will flow from within him" (John 7:38). Or that He told the Samaritan woman at the well, "The water I give [the believer] will become in him a spring of water welling up to eternal life" (John 4:14).

We need to understand that we live in fullness, that God has made us artesian wells! We come to church with God's fullness within, to contribute and share as well as to receive. And all week long the same fullness is within—nourishing, purifying, sustaining us. We're given a never-ending supply of Him!

Grey Christians think God is at work in healings but not in sicknesses.

Yet wonderful King Hezekiah said after his sickness, "Surely it was for my benefit that I suffered such anguish" (Isa. 38:17).

The Apostle Paul, who admired Timothy's "sincere faith" (2 Tim. 1:5), told him, "Use a little wine because of your stomach and your frequent illnesses" (1 Tim. 5:23).

And Paul himself, after praying three times to be freed from his "thorn in the flesh" (probably eye trouble) had this testimony:

> [God] said to me "My grace is sufficient for you, for my power is made perfect in weakness." Therefore I will boast all the more gladly about my weaknesses, so that Christ's power may rest on me. . . . For when I am weak, then I am strong (2 Cor. 12:9–10).

Grey Christians think God is at work in good times but not in bad.

Have you noticed Jonah's ups and downs (or should I say ins and outs)?

"The Lord provided a great fish" (Jon. 1:17) to rescue him from drowning.

"The Lord God provided a vine" (4:6) to shade him.

Then "God provided a worm" (4:7) to destroy the shade.

And then "God provided a scorching east wind, and the sun blazed on Jonah's head" (4:8).

The Lord provided them all: two goods, two bads.

Or think about Joseph; "the Lord was with him" in great times and in terrible times:

> His master saw that *the Lord was with him* and that the Lord gave him success in everything he did (Gen. 39:3).

> While Joseph was there in the prison, *the Lord was with him* (vv. 20–21).

Joseph lived serenely through it all because he understood that God was at work in everything in his life. So he

37

could say to his brothers who had abused him, "Don't be afraid. . . . You intended to harm me, but God intended it for good" (Gen. 50:20).

Indeed, you have that sweeping statement in Romans 8:28 that says flatly that God is at work in everything for you: "We know that in all things God works for the good of those who love him, who have been called according to his purpose."

Grey Christians don't see this. They go to church and maybe worship or serve the Lord with all their might, and then they go home and worry over things. Their Christianity is fractured and compartmentalized—and so are their hearts as well.

Grey Christians carve up their lives into "sacred" and "secular." They have the impression that prayer, Bible reading, church attendance, and "fellowship" are sacred acts that make God happy. Then there's eating, sleeping, lovemaking, working, recreation, and all the rest that are secular acts. For these they sort of apologize to God and look on them as necessary waste. And the upshot is that they feel uneasy most of the time and consider themselves "basically secular" Christians.

But the dogged, can't-get-away-from-it fact is that they're Christians—so they have to keep crossing back and forth all their lives between sacred and secular. And their inner hearts tend to break up into dividedness, purposelessness, frustration.

Says A. W. Tozer,

> They try to walk the tight rope between two kingdoms, and they find no peace in either. Their strength is reduced, their outlook is confused and their joy is taken from them.[1]

There is terrible danger in considering yourself a "basically secular" Christian! It gives you a low self-image, a feeling of weakness and failure, and a sense of standing on the threshold where it's only an easy step to a little drugs, a little sexual permissiveness, a little this or that.

Jeremiah lived among grey believers, and he cried,

---

1. *The Pursuit of God* (Harrisburg, PA: Christian Publications, 1948), 119.

My heart is broken. . .
because of the Lord
and his holy words.
The land is full of adulterers. . . .
"Even in my temple I find their wickedness,"
declares the Lord

(Jer. 23:9–11).

In that day, too, "consenting adults" behind closed doors were polluting society, and God cried,

Can anyone hide in secret places
so that I cannot see him? (v. 24).

Oh, my friend! It is radical and revolutionary and cleansing and purifying for you to see that *God is at work in everything*—and then adjust your life accordingly!

William Law (1686–1761) wrote in his book, *A Serious Call to a Devout and Holy Life,*

He . . . is the devout man [or we'll say woman] . . . who considers God in everything, who serves God in everything, who makes all the parts of [her] common life parts of piety, by doing everything in the name of God, and under such rules as are conformable to His glory.[2]

Jesus' life was like that. He'd given His whole human life to the Father (Heb. 10:5, 7), and the Father made no distinction between act and act. Jesus ate, He preached, He went to parties, He did miracles, He rested—and He said, "I always do what pleases him" (John 8:29).

If you read *Disciplines of the Beautiful Woman,* you may remember that I suggested a list of things to do when you're tempted to dawdle. Every one of those acts can be bright with the glory of God:

1. Exercise.
2. Memorize Scripture.
3. Look over your coming calendar and prepare what
   to wear.

2. (Philadelphia: Westminster, 1948), 1.

39

4. Give yourself a pedicure.
5. Write a list of your blessings.
6. Walk around your house critically: adjust, rearrange, throw out, give away.
7. Cook ahead for the freezer.
8. Cream yourself all over.
9. Read part of an important book.
10. Clean out your cosmetics drawer.
11. Write a letter to an old friend.
12. Do your nails.
13. Weed your garden.
14. Bring your recipe file up to date.
15. Encourage a Christian friend by telephone, someone you don't usually call.
16. Put all those old photos into albums.
17. Take a walk in the park.
18. Nap on a slant board, or with your feet up.
19. Have a prolonged time talking with God: partly on your knees, partly standing with hands raised, partly on your face before him on the floor.
20. Polish the silver.
21. Write a poem (don't be silly; everybody does).
22. Write your pastor an encouraging note.[3]

We may have done those activities as God's "beautiful women" to fill our time more profitably and live more efficiently. But now see a deeper dimension. In your thought life, in your heart life, judge each of those twenty-two acts. We are in God, and He is in us. *He in us* writes a letter to an old friend, weeds the garden, has a prolonged time of prayer! "It is the Father, living in me, who is doing his work" (John 14:10).

All is filled with God. All is in Him and before Him. All is done in humble submission to His will. "In all thy ways acknowledge him [in memorizing Scripture, in giving yourself a pedicure], and he shall direct thy paths" (Prov. 3:6, KJV). He will order your schedule; He will enjoy everything you do (and you will enjoy everything He does!) as you live in Him, and He in you. Your life is synchronized,

---

3. Ortlund, *Disciplines of the Beautiful Woman*, 65–66.

in harmony with His. His works are superimposed on yours—and yours on His!

And that's how He tells you to live (Col. 3:17)!

Open your eyes, my friend, and fill all your life with the brightness of the splendor of God! Live all your life seeing your powerful, loving Lord at work everywhere, in everything, in all your circumstances, in all your moments. Psalm 119:91 says, "All things serve [him]." Romans 11:36 says that "From him and through him and to him are all things."

Then nothing—nothing—is without God's wonderful meaning in it. "The earth is the Lord's, and everything in it" (Ps. 24:1). "The whole earth is full of his glory" (Isa. 6:3)! He knows when every sparrow falls, and He knows even the number of the hairs on your head (Matt. 10:29–30). He has established all governments (Rom. 13:1), and the hearts of all governmental rulers are in His hand, doing what He pleases (Prov. 21:1).

If God is truly at work in everything, you have brand new ground rules for living your Christian life.

Literally:

You're to cast all your anxiety on Him because He cares for you (1 Pet. 5:7).

You're not to repay anyone evil for evil; "'I will repay,' says the Lord" (Rom. 12:17–19).

You're not to fear anything, because He's with you (Ps. 23:4).

You'll never lack anything, because He's your Shepherd (Ps. 23:1).

When you pass through hard times, He'll see that they don't get the better of you (Isa. 43:2).

Says Hannah Whitall Smith,

[No action] can touch us except with [the Father's] knowledge and by His permission. It may be the sin of man that originates the action, and therefore the thing itself cannot be said to be the will of God; but by the time it reaches us it has become God's will for us, and must be accepted as directly from His hands.

No man or company of men, no power on earth or heaven, can touch that soul which is abiding in Christ, without first passing through His encircling presence and receiving the seal of His permission. If God be for us, it matters not who may be against us; nothing can disturb or harm us, except He shall see that it is best for us.[4]

Only if this is true does 1 Thessalonians 5:18 make sense: "Give thanks in all circumstances, for this is God's will for you in Christ Jesus."

God is at work in everything. Are you believing practically at this minute how great He is—how great He is *for you?* It should begin to relax your muscles even as you read.

"Be still," says the psalm.

"Let your hands hang down," says Hebrews.

Hear it again: you won't really rest and trust if you believe that He's only at work in some areas of your life, but that the rest is up to you. Do you have a grey mind, like most Christians, that mixes a little white and a little black and is confused, directionless, fractured?

Or will you *let God be God?*

---

4. *The Christian's Secret of a Happy Life* (Westwood, NJ: Barbour, 1985, originally published 1870), 151–152.

Now Work into Your Life
What You've Been Reading.

Write down in a list in your notebook each area of your life—how you spend your time. Following each of these areas write this prayer: "Lord, I give this area of my life to You. Do what You want with it. Subtract it or strengthen it or cleanse and purify it."

List your bad circumstances. Thank Him on paper for each one (1 Thess. 5:18)! Turn each one over to Him, asking Him as you write to heal your thought life concerning:

1. Your resentment
2. Your worry
3. Your tendency to take the matter into your own hands, or whatever.

Don't hurry.

Ask Him to give you an attitude of worship, praise, and rest each time one of these circumstances confronts you.

Remember, your living is between your ears!

Memorize Isaiah 26:3. Hold yourself accountable to someone who will hear you say it.

If you are reading this book in a small group, allow plenty of silence for this writing, and then share all that you're able of what you've written down. Pray for each other and memorize together.

7

Says Richard Foster, "In our day heaven and earth are on tiptoe waiting for the emerging of a Spirit-led, Spirit-intoxicated, Spirit-empowered people."[1]

I hope in the last few chapters you've been thrilling to the truth of God's possibilities for your life and His greatness on your behalf.

To believe it, to accept it, is the first step—but then you must walk on it and live in the light of it and be obedient to it, one day at a time. Then you will not only be "Spirit-empowered," but really and actually, as Foster said, "Spirit-led" and "Spirit-intoxicated," too. Oh, I do believe the time has come when God's people will grow their roots down deep in knowledge and grow their trunks and branches up tall in holiness and happiness! I think you and I have "come to the kingdom for such a time as this"!

You heard me say "you must" in that last paragraph. Did you catch it? And you're saying, "Hold it, Anne Ortlund! You've been saying that God's part is to do the work and our part is to rest and trust. Then what's this 'you must' business?"

I'm glad you asked that question. You're sharp to pick up on it and not let it pass!

The foundational truth is that there is God's side and there is our side. The work, the accomplishment, is only His. You in yourself can't be holy and happy, but Christ *can* be—in you and through you—and He will be if you ask Him to and let Him.

"The Lord will accomplish what concerns me" (Ps. 138:8, NASB).

---

1. *Celebration of Discipline* (San Francisco: Harper & Row, 1978), 150.

He establishes "the work of our hands" (Ps. 90:17)—our hands, His establishing.

Said Isaiah to the Lord, "All that we have accomplished you have done for us" (Isa. 26:12).

Here's a glove, empty and limp. I hold it up by its wrist and it can't wave, it can't pick up anything, it's helpless. Then I slide my hand into the glove, and my fingers fill all its fingers. Then it can seem full of dexterity and power!

"My, what a wonderful glove!" someone says. "It's so clever and gifted! It's brilliant!"

No, the glove is helpless in itself; it's the hand inside that's brilliant. And you know what? Any old out-of-fashion, funny-looking glove will do!

Your part is to relax and let Him work in you; His part is to achieve fabulous goals in you and for you. "He who trusts in himself is a fool, but he who walks in wisdom [in Christ] is kept safe" (Prov. 28:26).

Now, in the rest of the book I'm going to be mostly exhorting you and urging you—but you must understand it in the light of God's side and your side, or nothing much will happen. When your heart leaps up and you respond to something—"Oh, yes, that's what I want to be or do!"—then in the next breath say to God, "This, too, I surrender to You, Lord, to let You do the work in me. I rest in Your fabulous ability; I'm on tiptoe to see You do this wonderfully in my life. And I will give You the credit!"

Day by day, morning by morning, begin your walk with Him in the calm trust that *God is at work in everything.* George Mueller used to say, "It is my first business every morning to make sure that my heart is happy in God." He was right! It is your personal business, as a discipline of your heart, to learn to be peaceful and safe in God in every situation.

Some of my mornings I read this written in my notebook:

> The light of God surrounds me;
> The love of God enfolds me;
> The power of God protects me;
> The presence of God watches over me;
> Wherever I am, God is.

Remember, friend, where your real living is going on. In your thinking, in your reacting, in your heart of hearts—here is where your walk with God begins and continues. So when you start to move into trusting Him, *stay there*. Don't wander out again into worry and doubt!

Here's an old-fashioned illustration that's so good I can't think of a more modern one to replace it.[2] A piece of iron, in itself and by itself, is cold, black, hard, and ugly. But hold it in a furnace, and what a change takes place!

I saw this once with my own eyes at Lukens Steel Mill in Coatesville, Pennsylvania. The coldness was gone, the blackness was gone, the hardness was gone, the ugliness was gone—the iron had been transformed. The fire and the iron were still distinguishable from each other; the iron was certainly still iron. But as long as that iron was held in the fire, it had entered into a new experience, and it was hot and glowing and purified.

You ask me what I, Anne Ortlund, am in myself, and I can tell you that I'm "cold, black, hard, and ugly"! But as long as I remain in the fire of Christ, I'm hot and glowing and purified. From moment to moment it's my privilege to remain there, to "abide in Him"—and He Himself is my life and purity and power. Only He sets me free from the law of sin and death (Rom. 8:2)—but, oh, He does set me free!

Can I boast that this is true? Hey, I know very well what I am in myself.

Do I "know the Lord"? I've barely begun. Just the same, as Meister Eckhart said, "No one knows better what heat is than the man who is hot."[3]

Or do I mean I've come into some kind of sinless perfection? *I wish!* It would be my greatest delight, and it would make my life even happier and easier than it is now. But that rascal "self" keeps exploding out from the fire and has to be shoved back in again. Says 1 John 1:8, "If we claim to be without sin, we deceive ourselves and the truth is not in us."

---

2. Illustration taken from *The Message of Keswick* (London: Marshall, Morgan, and Scott, new edition 1957), 44.

3. *Meister Eckhart*, ed. James M. Clark (London: Thomas Nelson and Sons, 1957), 176.

But what a release, what a freedom indeed, to be delivered from trying to manage my own Christian life and to let Him take over! "The [person who] has discovered this secret of simple faith has found the key that will unlock the whole treasure-house of God!"[4]

I love J. B. Phillips's picture of this life in his translation of Romans 5:17: "Men by their acceptance of his . . . grace and righteousness should live all their lives like kings"!

Comments Oswald Sanders,

> What a fascinating picture of Christian living this vivid picture portrays: nobility, charm, authority, wealth, freedom. Our God invites us to believe that these spiritual qualities and prerogatives may and should be enjoyed by every child of the King of Kings. If we do not manifest and enjoy them, it is not because they are beyond our reach, but only because we are living below our privileges.[5]

I stop writing and sit a little taller. My heart shouts halleluia! As you read, are you joining me? Let's tell Him we never again want to live below our privileges—not when He has gone to such lengths to provide them, and not when He so delights in our receiving them!

4. Hannah Whitall Smith, *The Christian's Secret of a Happy Life* (Westwood, NJ: Barbour, 1985, originally published 1870), 42.

5. *Spiritual Maturity* (Chicago: Moody, 1962), 125.

Now Work into Your Life
What You've Been Reading.

Consider as yours, right now, the qualities Oswald Sanders says every child of the King should enjoy. In your notebook list each one, and then write beside them how they relate to Christ's own characteristics. Thank Him for each of these qualities and ask Him to live them out to the fullest in your life:
1. Nobility
2. Charm
3. Authority
4. Wealth
5. Freedom

If you're studying this book together in a small group, allow silence for this writing, and then share together as much of what you've written as you're able.

Follow with a time of joyous praise, perhaps with singing as well as prayer.

*Why God must do the work:
you and I are both weak and wicked.*

8

Now we need just two chapters to see how cold, black, hard, and ugly iron is—to get motivated to stay in that fire!

Are you willing to look hard at you and at me? Sin is such a big part of what God's Word has to say to you that to ignore it would be to ignore God. To shut your eyes to sin would be to stay outside the sheltering lighthouse of truth and to be exposed to all those satanic rocks.

You're aware of it: there are plenty of false religions today that never mention the word *sin,* and they're all out to make you one more convert on their list. But if you haven't examined the blackness, the awfulness of your sin so far in your Christian life, it's time.

That remarkable Christian Blaise Pascal (1623–1662) said, "We can only know God well when we know our own sin. And those who have known God without knowing their wretchedness have not glorified him, but have glorified themselves."[1]

What a description of today's Christianity!

(Am I rubbing the cat's fur the wrong way? Then turn around, cat! Popular ideas of the day don't nullify the Word of God. "Not at all! Let God be true, and every man a liar," Rom. 3:4.)

Christian, you must understand thoroughly what you are (remember the woodpecker!) if you're to *remain willing* to trust in God only for all His power in your life.

---

1. Sherwood E. Wirt, ed., *Spiritual Disciplines* (Westchester, IL: Crossway, 1983), 19. You may be interested to know that Pascal, who was sickly and only lived to be thirty-nine, was a physicist who discovered "Pascal's Law," which laid the foundation of modern hydraulics. He also invented the barometer and the calculator, the latter being the forerunner of today's computer. He was a Christian who, some have said, wrote the finest prose ever written by a Frenchman.

Jesus told about a fellow who went to the temple and prayed, "God, have mercy on me, a sinner." And because that man was willing to flat-out admit his sin, Jesus said, "I tell you that this man . . . went home justified [—totally justified—] before God" (Luke 18:13–14). Wow!

Grey Christians think they're a mixture of good and bad. Revelation 3:16 says that makes Jesus gag. Only because He pronounces us totally bad is He able to make us totally good—without any propping up or polishing up on our part at all.

In ourselves we are blacker than iron—black, black. Unless we see that, we will never hate sin and fear sin and be repelled by sin enough to stay in the fire. (Says Tozer, "The Holy Spirit is first of all a moral flame.")

I began this book telling about Dr. George Gallup's last poll, which reveals the fact that Christians today are at a dangerous crossroads—high in religious fervor, low in knowledge—exposed and vulnerable.

I see another trend—moral deterioration. How can I say that, when earlier I said we're ready for broad-scale renewal? Because both trends are true; that's why we're indeed teetering in the balance.

But there's no doubt of it at all: we *are* deteriorating morally. With so many out of the fire, we're cooling off and getting blacker. I see evangelical Christianity passing from the wonderful height of its acceptance *IN* this world to the depth of its acceptance *OF* this world.

I see how when liberalism waned and we evangelicals rose to popularity and were listened to—we could have given our authentic message and cried to the world, "Repent! Be radically cleansed of your sin! Receive Jesus Christ's purity and holiness for your lives!"

But instead, in that time of golden opportunity, we lost our courage. We became embarrassed by our "separation" from the world, and we cozied up to it and joined it. We Madison-Avenue-trivialized our glorious gospel. And we stained ourselves with the world's adulteries and fornications.

I heard a respected old pastor comment recently at our lunch table that just as in the last twenty years Christians have accepted and gotten comfortable with adultery (through divorce), so in the next twenty years they will equally accept and get comfortable with abortion and homosexuality. I see it happening already: church families are secretly murdering little fetuses within their single daughters and ignoring the fact that their church musician is gay because he "helps the people to worship. . . ."

We're getting colder, blacker, harder, uglier! We must weep; we must mourn! We must hate with a holy hatred our blackness, our sin, our ugliness, our coldness, our hardness—that wrenches and tears our Father's heart and makes the pain of Jesus' cross go on and on!

> None of the ransomed ever knew
> How deep were the waters crossed;
> Nor how dark was the night that the Lord passed through
> Ere He found His sheep that was lost.[2]

* * *

> For all that He suffered,
>   in Gethsemane,
>   in Gabbatha,
>   in Calvary,
> For the pain,
>   the shame,
>   the curse, of the cross,
> That He deigned to be betrayed
>   and that by His own disciple,
> That He deigned to be sold,
>   and that for thirty pieces of silver;
>   to be troubled in His mind,
>   to be weary,
>   to fear,
>   to be exceeding sorrowful, even unto death,
>   to be in an agony,
>   with strong crying,
>   and tears,

---

2. Elizabeth C. Clephane (1830–1869), "The Ninety and Nine."

to sweat great drops of blood, . . .
to be left alone,
and denied by Peter,
and that with an oath,
and a curse;
to be subjected to the powers of darkness,
to be laid hands on,
taken as a thief,
bound,
carried away,
hurried to Annas,
Caiaphas,
Pilate,
Herod,
Pilate the second time,
the Praetorium,
Gabbatha,
the cross.
Thou that wast silent before the judge,
restrain my tongue.
Thou that didst deign to be bound,
restrain my hands. . . .
In that Thou was struck with the palm of the hand
before Annas,
accused before Caiaphas,
attacked by false witnesses,
condemned for blasphemy . . .
stricken,
spit upon,
reviled,
blasphemed:
Thy head was crowned with thorns,
and struck with the reed,
Thine eyes dim with tears,
Thine ears filled with reviling,
Thy mouth given to drink of gall and vinegar,
Thy face marred with spitting,
Thy back ploughed with the scourge,
Thy neck bent down with the cross, . . .
Thy feet pierced with nails,

53

Thy heart oppressed with grief,
Thy side pierced with the lance,
Thy Blood flowing . . .
Thy Soul in bitterness,
   and Thy cry of agony,
    "Eli, Eli!" . . .
Thou, Who didst deign
   that Thy glorious head should be wounded,
   forgive thereby whatever, by the senses of my
    head, I have sinned.
That Thy holy hands should be pierced,
forgive thereby, whatever I have done amiss
   by unlawful touch,
   or illicit operation.
That Thy precious side should be opened,
forgive thereby whatever I have offended
   by lawless thoughts,
   in the ardor of passion.
That Thy blessed feet should be riven,
forgive thereby whatever I have done
   by the means of feet swift to evil. . . .
And I, too, Lord, am wounded in soul;
   behold the multitude,
   the length, the breadth, the depth of my wounds;
   and by Thine, heal mine.[3]

Let us pray separately—you, reader, and me—in our shame for our having done this to our Lord. Let us ask Him to forgive our unwashed praises before Him, our sillinesses, our ignorances.

Let us see how our coldness, hardness, blackness, ugliness becomes colder, harder, blacker, uglier—unless in terror we wrench ourselves free and rush to His precious fire! Let us see again in Romans 1 the progression of moral ruin:

1. Knowing God
2. But not praising and glorifying Him as God,
3. Not giving Him thanks,
4. Becoming futile in our thinking,

---

3. *The Private Devotions of Lancelot Andrewes* (New York: World, 1956), 185–190.

5. Becoming darkened in heart,
6. Becoming idolaters,
7. Becoming lesbians and gays,
8. Practicing every known sin,
9. Having pleasure in others who do the same. . . .

God our Father,
Lord Jesus Christ our Savior,
Holy Spirit, purifying, white-hot Fire,
    We rush to You.

Now Work into Your Life
What You've Been Reading.

1. Let us weep and mourn for our sins: write to God, on paper, confessing to Him. (You may want to put your confession on a separate sheet of paper, read 1 John 1:9, and then completely tear up your list. Those sins are gone forever!)

2. Read Isaiah 63:1–10 again and meditate on how much He loved us, His enemies (Rom. 5:10). Thank Him, thank Him—writing in your notebook as eloquently as He will give you words.

If you are studying this book in a small group, allow a time of silence for the writing of number 1. Then read and discuss Isaiah 63:1–10 and spend much time in prayer together for thanksgiving.

9

You must commit yourself to moral purity. No matter where you're starting—from this moment on, you must. First Thessalonians 3:13 says this begins when you "strengthen your heart," so do it right now. Say "yes" to 1 Thessalonians 4:3–8, which begins, "It is God's will that you should be holy."

You don't need to pray to see if it's His will for you to have sex with that wonderful Christian you love and are soon to marry; for your church to hire that homosexual who's such a glorious musician; for you to wed that respected, long-time Christian whose divorced wife is still alive . . . for you to embrace fornication, homosexuality, or adultery in any form—all defined in 1 Thessalonians 4:3 by the Greek word *porneia,* from which comes our word *pornography.*

"Abstain," says God. He doesn't say "Be careful" or "Pray about it"—He says, "Abstain! Run from it! Don't touch it! Have nothing to do with it!"

Stay pure and blameless. If you don't, God will suffer most of all. (When we sin, *God* loses!) But He will also let you share in His suffering by punishing you (1 Thess. 4:4–8)—through anxieties, conflicts, guilt, disease, or worse.

(A telltale sign of moral weakness and susceptibility to temptation is excessive interest in the physical—food, clothes, fitness—and a weak interest in the spiritual—prayer, the Word, fellowship, ministry. Judge yourself before the Lord.)

Now, let me picture for you as strongly, as vividly as I can that God wants you to stay away from sin. Read carefully a lesson from history.

Practically from the first, Amalek was an enemy of God.

He was the grandson of Esau by a concubine (Gen. 36:12), and his tribesmen were the first to try to hinder Israel from escaping the Egyptians (Exod. 17:8–16). For that reason, on the spot God promised Moses that He'd eventually destroy the Amalekites (Exod. 17:14–16; Deut. 25:17–19).

During the following centuries, the Amalekites fought God's people at every opportunity—plundering them, killing them, hassling them, oppressing them—until finally God told King Saul, in effect, "Enough! The sins of the Amalekites have reached full measure, and it's time to wipe them and all their possessions off the face of the earth" (1 Sam. 15:1–3).

Unfortunately, Saul didn't happen to share God's views. So he wiped off the face of the earth the part of the Amalekites that didn't look good to him—and spared the rest for his personal use, hoping God wouldn't notice.

But here came God's prophet Samuel! Sounding as hearty and business-as-usual as he could, Saul chirped, "The Lord bless you! I have carried out the Lord's instructions" (1 Sam. 15:13).

"What then," interrogated the prophet sarcastically, "is this bleating of sheep in my ears? What is this lowing of cattle that I hear?" (v. 14). Saul hadn't fooled him a bit!

And because King Saul didn't hate what God hated and didn't destroy what God wanted destroyed, God took away his crown and his reign.

God hasn't changed today. You must hate what He hates and destroy what He wants destroyed. He knows the damage these enemies do to His children, the hurt and anguish they cause to His precious ones, and when He says "kill them"—*do it!*

Colossians 3:5–8 is this kind of command. God says,

> Put to death, therefore, whatever belongs to your earthly nature: sexual immorality, impurity, lust, evil desires and greed, which is idolatry. . . . Rid yourselves of all such things as these: anger, rage, malice, slander, and filthy language from your lips.

Friend, if you don't think they're as awful as God thinks they are—and if you let some of them hang around instead of ruthlessly killing them—understand right now that, as He did to Saul, God will remove your stature, He'll cut down your influence, He'll give you disgrace.

Look carefully at these things listed in Colossians 3, and ask yourself if you hate each one as God hates them. Do you let any of them hang around? Do you let them coexist in your life as if they were acceptable? Are you tolerating God's enemies?

Nehemiah didn't. When he came back from a trip and found Tobiah put up as a guest in God's house—Tobiah, who'd been God's enemy from the start—do you know what Nehemiah did? He literally threw out all Tobiah's stuff with his own two hands and had the room cleaned up and restored (Neh. 13:6–9).

Listen, the world is full of Christians who pass around little "spiritual" books and go to Bible classes and say "praise the Lord" a lot—at the same time showing no desire to put to death the characteristics of their earthly natures.

To people like these, the love of Jesus crucified is pure sentimentality. And whether they know it or not, they are utterly without power in their lives.

True Christianity costs. It costs plenty. You kick out all the enemies. You put to death everything God tells you to put to death.

Lust must go—wham!

Greed, likewise—pow!

Filthy language isn't funny—kill it!

And if any of these enemies comes to and raises his head, bash him again.

To love God and to please Him is worth everything, everything. Your sexual immorality must go, your evil desires and greed must go, your anger must go, your malice must go, your slander must go. All of them must go—forever! Be ruthless. Whatever the sins are that right now make you feel guilty and uneasy—hate them! Murder them! Get them once and for all out of your life.

And don't you dare read these words just to have read

one more Christian book—just for a little evangelical tickling and entertainment. Let these words jar you to instant obedience.

What lurking thing are you hosting, coddling, hanging on to, putting up with? You know how your Lord Christ feels about it.

You say you're "only a woman," and it doesn't even seem ladylike to think so tough?

General Sisera was an enemy of God, the commander of a Canaanite army which cruelly abused God's people, Israel. So Jael—"only a woman," "just a housewife"—lured him into her tent, offered him rest and a snack, got him covered up and cozy and off to sleep, quietly picked up a tent peg and a hammer, and—THUNG! She drove that thing right through his temple (Judg. 4:4–21).

You know what sin you have to put to death.

Do it with all your strength.

Personally.

Quickly.

Now Work into Your Life What You've Been Reading.

Confessions, like trash collections, have to be regular and thorough. The alternative to continual repentance and confession is:
1. Guilty feelings, man's greatest underminer, which lead to . . .
2. The crippling, addicting habit of lying to oneself ("I'm not all that bad"), which leads to . . .
3. A self-deception of being partially good, partially able, which leads to . . .
4. False starts, "new year's resolutions," with no power of implementation, so that each produces more disillusionment and hopelessness than the one before, which lead to . . .
5. Manufactured excuses ("Oh, well, we're all human"), blaming others or circumstances, and lowered expectations of future performance, which lead to . . .
6. A general, habitual malaise due to low self-esteem and self-pity, and a temptation to further sins.

In contrast,
1. Repentance and confession look squarely at reality. ("I am a vile, helpless, hopeless sinner, worse than I know, and my personal attitudes and actions are repugnant to a pure and holy God.")
2. Repentance and confession submit to God's own assessment of the situation: that He isn't mad at you, that He cares about you totally and considers you too precious to lose, that He was willing—even eager—to go to the Cross to redeem you.
3. Repentance and confession qualify you for His immediate and complete forgiveness and cleansing from all your sins, both known to you and unknown (1 John 1:9), and the throwing over you of Christ's robe of absolute righteousness in His eyes (Isa. 61:10).

61

4. Repentance and confession, then, as a way of life, cause you to know very well what you are in yourself but to walk in the light, balanced and with head up (1 John 1:7). You live not in your flesh but in the Spirit (Rom. 8:5–9). Your human tendency is death—but you are alive with life (Rom. 8:10–11)!

Get on your face before Him (why not literally?). Confess to Him your sins, your repentance, and your total acceptance of His cleansing. Don't hurry the process.

If you're in a group, this can be one of the most meaningful and life-changing sessions you'll ever have. Get at least on your knees and be as honest with Him before each other as His Spirit controls and allows in His delicate taste and wisdom. (There is far more you will confess to Him only in private.)

He will make it a holy and cleansing time.

Break the back of your own ego.

10

Jesus said, "Blessed are the meek, for they will inherit the earth" (Matt. 5:5). Blessed—happy, to be congratulated—are those who understand exactly what they are and don't try by pretense or posing to deny it or cover it.

Grey Christians aren't much into meekness. To them it sounds weird—and not very desirable. Of course they love the "inheriting the earth" part; coming into a huge piece of real estate sounds terrific. ("The whole earth? Wow!") And they say they take God's Word as truth. But getting an inheritance by becoming *meek?* In reality they shrug off the parts of the Bible that don't have a good, twentieth-century-American ring to them.

Then our Christ, in love, explains to us more what He means by meekness:

> Come unto me, all ye that labour and are heavy laden, and I will give you rest. Take my yoke upon you, and learn of me; for I am meek and lowly in heart: and ye shall find rest unto your souls. For my yoke is easy, and my burden is light (Matt. 11:28–30, KJV).

Do you know what your burden is—the one that Jesus wants to remove? It's a burden you manufacture all by yourself between your ears. And most people carry it, are "heavy laden" by it, are dragged down and depressed and discouraged and exhausted by it all their lives.

It's the burden of ego.

How much emotional energy do you spend protecting yourself from every possible slight, challenging every word spoken by either friend or enemy which demeans you, cringing under every cool look, tossing at night because someone else seemed preferred over you? How much emotional energy do you spend trying to doctor up your image and "look good," trying to say only what's "cool," trying to do only what's accepted, trying to appear only in a way that will make you admired, trying to sustain a subtle publicity campaign that says you are more, do more, have more . . . ?

Exhausting, isn't it?

It's a cruel, crushing burden, and it never lets up. It never lets you relax a minute to recoup. It wears away your strength, your morale, your life. We may call it "stress," but its real name is "ego."

Ego may be open or subtle, worldly or Christianized. It may mean smashing enough faces and brains to wow the world of boxing. It may mean taking over enough companies to wow the corporate world of business. It may mean getting enough church members or adherents to wow the religious world. Or individually, memorizing the most verses, visiting the most shut-ins, teaching the biggest Bible class—whatever makes the rest say "wow!"

Or ego may mean writhing and seething because you *haven't* made it to the top: you lost the match, your company was outclassed, your ministry is struggling. . . .

Ego keeps you forever tense and dissatisfied, forever in agony lest someone else appear better, smarter, richer, more liked, more successful, more admired, more spiritual, more "blessed." . . .

Ego is a terrible, terrible burden.

Jesus says, "Let me give you rest. Learn of Me. I am meek!"

Meekness is the opposite of ego with its pretense, pride, competition.

"I will give you rest," He says. "Accept the blessed relief of being only what you are. Then I can do it all!

"Quit pretending. Quit striving. My dear child, quit trying to be some cocky little god competing with Me— maybe, worst of all, some cocky little *religious* god. Come down off your silly, rickety throne.

"Only my Father is worthy of a throne! Bow to Him only, and give Him all the glory, and let Him be all and do all, in you and for you!"

When you think of it, that's how Jesus Himself was meek. He was willing to do only the Father's will—to do only what the Father told Him to do and say only what the Father told Him to say.

Meekness sounds awful, though, to grey Christians— like they'd come out losers, nerds, nothings.

That's the devil's lie.

What made Satan fall in the first place? It was his determination to exalt his own ego. He swore,

> I will ascend to heaven;
> I will raise my throne
> Above the stars of God . . .
> I will make myself like the Most High (Isa. 14:13–15).

Satan wanted to be "self-made"! God wouldn't have it (Luke 10:18).

Satan, in his fallen state, tried to tempt the Lord Jesus to do the same thing—exalt His ego:

> The devil led him up to a high place and showed him in an instant all the kingdoms of the world. And he said to him, "I will give you all their authority and splendor. . . . If you worship me, it will all be yours" (Luke 4:5–7).

Jesus refused and instead took the meek way—to the cross. He really did put His head in the noose, didn't He? He walked into it with His eyes wide open!

And did His meekness make Him a loser? Did the Cross make Jesus Christ a nerd, a nothing?

No, no, no, no! Because He resolutely turned His back on ego and chose meekness, in the end all will bow down to Him—not just those kingdoms of the earth that Satan displayed to Him, but every knee "in heaven and on earth and under the earth" (Phil. 2:10)—more, infinitely more.

Long before the devil tempted Jesus, he also tempted Eve to exalt her ego: "When you eat of [the fruit] your eyes will be opened, and you will be like God" (Gen. 3:5).

Unlike Jesus, however, Eve obeyed Satan and *fell*. She didn't go up, she went down. And she fell so far that the magnitude of her fall dragged the whole human race down with her. Talk about a crash!

Now, "he who has an ear, let him hear what the Spirit says" (Rev. 2:7). Listen to the quiet voice of love, with its sweet reasonableness, wanting the best for you (a "best" so good we can't imagine it):

> Come to me, all you who are weary and burdened, and I will give you rest.

"I have no desire," He says, "for you to go on being crushed under this great burden of trying to be what you're not and trying not to be what you are. Let it roll off. Let it go. What an enormous yoke it is! My dear, you're all exhausted from posing, from exaggerating, from hiding, from trying to *appear* instead of just *being*. Let Me help you take this ugly thing off. Poor child! Here, put on Mine instead":

> Take my yoke upon you and learn of me, for I am [meek] and humble in heart, and you will find rest for your souls. For my yoke is easy, and my burden is light.

Says Christ, "My name is 'I AM WHO I AM,' as Exodus 3:14 puts it. I don't try to defend Myself or to appear to be different than I am. Satan, on the other hand, 'masquerades as an angel of light' (2 Cor. 11:14), and all his followers try to do the same. It's part of their death struggle; they're on their way out.

"I never had to do that," He continues, "and neither do My children. You are who you are: accepted in the Beloved, precious in My sight, and in the process of becoming perfect as I am perfect—a process so sure that I already see you that way!

"Isn't that enough? Aren't you satisfied with My plan?"

> Humble yourselves, therefore, under God's mighty hand, that he may lift you up in due time (1 Pet. 5:6).

"Lift you up in due time"?
Lord—like maybe, "inherit the earth"?

Now Work into Your Life
What You've Been Reading.

1. In your notebook, writing your new determination to God, take off the burden of ego you've been wearing. List and describe the characteristics of your personal ego, and after each description write, "Right now, Lord, I let this roll off." At the end of this process deliberately sit taller and take a long, deep, fresh breath of air.

2. Then describe on paper to your wonderful Christ your action of putting on His easy, comfortable yoke of meekness and honesty of heart. Do it with eager enjoyment and prayer, in the power of the Spirit. Understand how much He's enjoying this, too! He loves you very much.

If you are studying this book in a small group allow silence for the individual writing of number 1. Then in conversational prayer describe to Christ what you see of His own yoke and express in prayer, with thanksgiving, your act of putting it on.

If this isn't easy before each other, understand that learning to walk together "in the light" (exposed, knowable, open) as He is in the light is your only way to true fellowship together and to cleansing (1 John 1:7). Christ in you (remember the hand in the glove?) will be the help you need to begin a new habit—of being yourself!

11

God, your dear Father, is the One before whom you humble yourself. As you get to know Him, you rush to Him not only to get "hot, glowing, and purified," but because He's so wonderful to come to!

He's the north star from which we all get our bearings. He's the tuning fork by which we derive our pitch. He's the fact of facts. He's the beginning and the end of all. He's the magnetic field of attraction to which everything is drawn.

We come to Him because frankly it's such an easier way to live, and so much more fun—exhilarating, challenging, important, noble. Jesus Christ is Square One, and anything not related to Him is ultimately meaningless and futile.

And yet we know what it is to withdraw from His fire and start getting occupied again with ourselves and bugged with each other, fidgeting with our "self-images" and trying unsuccessfully to play "I'm okay, you're okay."

We know what it's like to "worship" Him when we're too far from the fire. We get very aware of shutting our eyes and raising our hands and noticing with sidewise glances who *isn't* shutting and raising—or very smugly aware that *our* kind of church is certainly not the sort to get into shutting and raising. . . . God help us all.

When we get back into the fire, we're aware of God again —and suddenly we're humble! We see who we really are, and we're just as embarrassed as that fellow Jesus talked about (Luke 14:7–9) who glided gracefully to the best seat at the wedding and had to be asked to move.

We'll suddenly understand and identify with the Pharisee at the temple (Luke 18:11) who "prayed about himself, 'God, I thank you that I am not like all other men— robbers, evildoers. . . .'"—posturing there, making a fool of himself, and absolutely unaware that his hearers couldn't decide whether to laugh or throw up.

When we get back in the fire, when we're abiding in our blessed Lord, then when He tells us to humble ourselves— hey, we won't think it's some big-deal spiritual project; we'll know it's just common sense.

Lectured Evelyn Underhill at one of her retreats,

> If we and our interesting little souls and their needs and experiences are still in the foreground of the spiritual land- scape; if we are still making man the measure of things; if our thanksgiving is complacent and all about our being such splendid creatures . . . we are not yet clear of that unreal, anthropocentric, man-centered religious world which is from beginning to end the creation of human pride.[1]

As she says later, "He and His will matter—not us and our satisfaction and enlightenment!"

Meister Eckhart in the thirteenth century said it more simply:

> Whoever wishes to receive from above must be below in true humility. . . . Nothing is given to him who is not truly below, nor does he receive anything at all, not even the smallest thing. If you consider yourself in the least, or anything or anyone, you are not below, and you will not receive anything. But if you are altogether below, you will receive fully and completely.[2]

Do you wonder what books of today ring with such bedrock truth that they'll be cherished seven hundred years from now? Read with conviction these further words of Eckhart, written so long ago:

> Some persons want to see God with their own eyes, just as they see a cow; and want to love God, just as they love a

---

1. *The Mount of Purification* (London: Longman, Green, 1960), p. 22.
2. *Meister Eckhart*, 174.

cow. You love it for the sake of its milk and cheese and for your own profit.

So do all those who love God for the sake of outward wealth or inward consolation; they merely love their own advantage. It is the plain truth that everything you put foremost in your thoughts and purposes that is not God Himself, however good it may be, cannot fail to be a hindrance to you on your way to the highest truth.[3]

Of course he's absolutely right on both scores—that we must come humbly and that we mustn't come just for what we'll get out of it.

But do you think that's the end of the matter as far as God's concerned? Not on your life!

Look at the prodigal son in Luke 15.

He *did* come to his father humbly; his planned speech said, "I am no longer worthy to be called your son; make me like one of your hired men" (v. 19).

But he also came for what he would get out of it; he said to himself, "How many of my father's hired men have food to spare, and here I am starving to death! I will set out and go back to my father. . . ." (vv. 17–18).

Both issues his father impatiently brushed off. Hired man? His father saw him coming a long way off, ran to him, threw his arms around him, and kissed him—the Greek verb is continuous, meaning he kept on kissing him and kissing him!

"Eat the servants' food? Are you kidding? I'm ordering a feast with everything and the very best clothes for you and—let's see, you need a really handsome ring to complete the look. . . ."

My friend, *our* part is to humble ourselves in sincerest penitence before Almighty God. But He is such a lover— and He loves to love! He will insist on raising you to look right into His eyes—insist that you have fellowship with Him heart to heart as best friends, His mind having fellowship with your mind on ever deepening levels; insist that you have everything you need and more, as befitting

---

3. Ibid., 147–48.

one favored by the great God of all gods and King above all.

Do you know that your groveling before Him even makes Him impatient? Making ourselves nothing in order to make Him everything really turns Him off. (Ray and I understand that; I can't abide for him to put himself down, and neither can he stand it when I belittle myself. That's the way lovers are.)

It *is* our place to remember what we are, in ourselves, in order to appreciate all that we are in Christ! But self-occupation (whether we're saying "I'm wonderful" or "I'm a louse") is sin, and God won't have it.

Think about Moses. God planned a fabulous walk through life with Moses. But when He began to broach the subject to Moses—

> Go down, Moses,
>   'Way down in Egypt land;
> Tell ol' Pharaoh,
>   "Let my people go!"

—Moses began making objecting noises: "Who am I . . . ?" (Exod. 3:11); "Suppose I . . ." (3:13); "what if . . ." (4:1); and then just outright, "O Lord, I have never been eloquent. . . . I am slow of speech and tongue" (4:10).

God's answer was quick: "Who gave man his mouth? . . . Is it not I, the Lord? Now go; I will help you speak" (4:11–12).

And when Moses was still self-demeaning, God's anger "burned against" him (4:14). He can't stand to have His cherished children reviled by others or even by themselves.

His side, your side: understand the difference.

You stumble to the door of a castle—ragged, filthy, embarrassed, insecure. . . .

And when you go in, the King Himself eagerly takes over. He welcomes you with all His heart, bathes and clothes you gorgeously, and makes you the guest of honor at a royal feast.

But *you must receive it all.* Don't you dare sit in a corner miserable because you're remembering who you are and where you came from. That wouldn't honor your Host! He loves you, and He did it all to give you the time of your life.

And *you must stay there.* Well, who would be so rude—or so foolish—as to leave?

"The king has brought [you] into his chambers" (Song of Sol. 1:4). The friends are standing around rejoicing and delighting in you.

Relax! Enjoy! Forever!

Now Work into Your Life
What You've Been Reading.

In your notebook, make a list of all that you've come into as an adopted child of the King. If you need help, look at Ephesians 1:3–14. Thank Him, in your own words, for each thing He's given you.

If you are studying this book in a small group, read and discuss Ephesians 1:3–14 together, writing in your notebook all the aspects you see there of your new position in Christ. Then have a time of thanksgiving in prayer together.

Chapter 12

Move out of the world of "things";
move into the real world —

12

It's fabulously true, my friend, that the King of heaven has brought you into His chambers and endowed you with every treasure He can assemble, and that He asks you only to believe and enjoy and let your new life become more and more real to you!

But there's one more important clue to making sure that the awful burden of ego is lifted from your back, so that you're truly freed to receive all your royal Sovereign wants you to have.

Do you remember the scene in the musical, *My Fair Lady*, when Professor Higgins took the flower girl Eliza Doolittle off the streets and had his maids scrub her and burn her clothes so he could give her new ones? Remember the way she howled? She was comfortable with her dirt, and she liked her old clothes! Many a Christian woman (man, too!) says by her attitude, "I prefer the old rags and trinkets that I've acquired all by myself. They're mine!"

Albert Edward Day has an important insight here:

> Left to itself, the ego is persistent in acquiring and keeping. Sharing is not one of its passions. . . .
>
> Giving is not a trait of the ego. Owning is! "Mine" is its dearest adjective. "Keep" is its most beloved verb.
>
> The ego is possessive. Its possessiveness in property manifests itself as stinginess, miserliness, greed. Its possessiveness of people makes jealous friends, husbands, wives, parents.
>
> Most persons who are possessive never recognize the fact. So complete is the domination of the ego that it is unconscious.[1]

---

1. *Discipline and Discovery* (Nashville: Upper Room, 1977), 80.

Woe to him, exclaims Jeremiah, who props up his ego with, for instance, real estate:

> He says, "I will build myself a great palace
> with spacious upper rooms."
> So he makes large windows in it,
> panels it with cedar
> and decorates it in red.
> Does it make you a king
> to have more and more cedar? (Jer. 22:14–15).

That's a probing question: "Does it make you a king . . . ?" Or we would say, "Does it make you a queen . . . ?" The world says yes. God says no:

> Do not worry about your life, what you will eat or drink; or about your body, what you will wear. . . . Look at the birds . . . they do not sow or reap or store away in barns, and yet your heavenly Father feeds them. . . . See how the lilies of the field grow. They do not labor or spin. Yet I tell you that not even Solomon in all his splendor was dressed like one of these. If that is how God clothes the grass of the field, . . . will he not much more clothe you? (Matt. 6:25–30).

If God clothes the grass so gorgeously, He may see fit to give you a big house, too—paneled with cedar and decorated in red! Then again, He may not. But the point is not what you have or don't have! That's not what makes you a queen; *God* makes you a queen (Rev. 5:10, KJV)! *You are a queen* in any case, not by your work, but by His work.

The point is not, I say, what you have materially or don't have. *Your living is between your ears*—whether you trust this area of your life, like the rest, to Him, or whether you're fascinated by "things," doting on them, worried over them, trying to get more of them, equating them with status.

"Do not worry," says Matthew 6:25.
"Why do you worry?" says Matthew 6:28.
"Do not worry," says Matthew 6:31.
"Do not worry," says Matthew 6:34.

My brother Bobby and I used to play marbles on our living room rug. He always won, but I was a sucker and we'd keep playing until Mother called us to dinner.

We never thought to ask each other, "Do you think we'll get any dinner tonight? Do you think Daddy brought home any food? Do you think Mother cooked it? What if they've forgotten us? What if they've decided not to feed us any more? Should we have done something to earn it, so they'd keep giving it to us?"

Hey, we were their *kids*. Our job was to play marbles, and their job was to supply the grub!

If you get momentarily anxious over finances, picture yourself a little kid playing on the floor. Your job is basically just to wait for the dinner call. This is not to say you shouldn't work and have a sense of responsibility (2 Thess. 3:6–13), but *your source of supply is not your paycheck from your work.* Your source of supply is your heavenly Father, who knows better than you do what you need (Matt. 6:32) and has promised to supply just the right amount.

Ego is very uncomfortable with this plan. Satan whispers through your ego, "Ridiculous! You'll probably be a pauper. Say you trust Him if it makes you feel better, but you'd probably also better do a little scrambling on your own!"

Then he triumphantly throws in his counterfeit Bible verse, which he made up all by himself: "Don't forget—God helps those who help themselves." And he grins, thinking of the millions of grey Christians who believe his "verse."

Is Satan right? Will you be poor?

Think about how God made you so thoughtfully and how He cherishes you, and think about how lovers delight in giving to the ones they love. Think about how the father clothed the prodigal son he loved so much. Think about how Matthew 6:30 says, "If that is how God clothes the grass of the field, . . . will he not *much more* clothe you?"

"Well," you say, "what about all the poor Christians and even starving ones around the world?"

The former president of World Vision told me, when I asked him outright, that he had never heard of a Christian anywhere starving to death. He said he knew stories that sometimes they get very hungry—and then when they pray they're thrilled to see God come through for them. Dr. Wilbur Smith used to say that in the last two thousand years of world history, those nations which have regularly repeated "give us this day our daily bread" have never experienced starvation.

Standards of living differ, expectations differ, needs differ—but no child of our Father has ever known Him to go back on His often-repeated promise to take care of His own.

> I was young and now I am old, [wrote David,]
>   yet I have never seen the righteous forsaken
>   or their children begging bread (Ps. 37:25).

So how wrong is Satan? Does God want you rich? Well, could your ego handle it? God is most concerned about what happens in the disciplines of your heart.

"Trust Me," He says. "Trust Me. Trust Me."

And then He gives you one dynamite, measurable, black-and-white way to trust Him—by regular, planned, sacrificial giving to Him! Writes Albert Day,

> Because of the possessiveness of the ego, the practice of generosity is very significant. It is a denial, a repudiation of the ego. Faithfully practiced, generosity weakens the ego's authority.[2]

Giving is the way to riches, because you can handle the riches when your ego has been gotten out of the way:

> Give, and it will be given to you. A good measure, pressed down, shaken together and running over, will be poured into your lap. For with the measure you use [in giving], it will be measured to you (Luke 6:38).

But will God give you all this just so you can more and more feather your own nest? Says 2 Corinthians 9:11, "You will be made rich in every way so that you can be generous on every occasion."

---

2. Ibid., 80.

My friend, if this is the life you want—this life of trust and rest and richness in Christ—deliberately turn your back on the touchable, material world and concentrate on the *real* world.

The real world is everywhere around you. It's not a future world; it's right now on all sides of you—more stable, more lasting, and of far greater value than the world you've been temporarily looking at:

> There is something in man which longs for the Perfect and Unchanging, and is sure, in spite of the confusions, the evils, the rough and tumble of life, that the Perfect and the Unchanging is the real.[3]

> So we fix our eyes not on what is seen, but on what is unseen. For what is seen is temporary, but what is unseen is eternal (2 Cor. 4:18).

If you open your eyes to the real world of God, to rest in it and enjoy it, trusting Christ and having fellowship with Him moment by moment, more and more, you'll find you've become more truly human and sensitive and alive.

If you live in the grey world of trying to combine God and materialism, you'll become more and more earthly, self-centered, dull, flabby, bloated, insensitive, and out of touch. The choice is up to you.

If you choose aliveness in God, you won't withdraw *out of* the world; you'll love it, with a cleansed and pure love, and want to serve it more than ever before. Still, in your heart there'll be a sense of separation, of detachment, knowing that world is fading away (Isa. 51:6).

"Oh, pastor," exclaimed a woman once to Charles Spurgeon, "I'm afraid the world is coming to an end!"

"Never mind, my dear," that great preacher answered. "We can get along without it."

Friend, turn from being consumed by fabrics and furniture and food. Move out of obsession with that external world into the real world—where your heart is a bona fide

---

3. Underhill, *Mount of Purification*, 239.

naturalized citizen, and where your thinking processes and habits are becoming more and more at home.

But then, when you consciously begin to "live and move and have [your] being" (Acts 17:28) in the real world, you come to an amazing discovery. You begin to understand that "things" are not only external to you; they're actually subservient to you. You thought you were moving away from them—but that was only between your ears. Material things are still available. They are created by God just so He can meet your external needs while you give your focus and attention to what is real.

When, in your mind, you're freed from possessing, then you possess all things!

All things are yours . . . and ye are Christ's; and Christ is God's (1 Cor. 3:21, 23, KJV).

Seek first his kingdom and his righteousness, and all these things will be given to you as well (Matt. 6:33).

He who did not spare his own Son, but gave him up for us all—how will he not also, along with him, graciously give us all things? (Rom. 8:32).

Now Work into Your Life What You've Been Reading.

1.   Right now read out loud to Him this prayer: "O Lord, open my eyes to the world of reality! Open my eyes to see what You see, to love what You love, to hate what You hate, and to use with ease what You give me to use."

2.   Read Hebrews 1:14 and then read aloud this prayer: "O Lord, give me the habit of continual awareness of the angels assigned to serve me. Make me grateful for them."

3.   Read 2 Kings 6:15–17 and then read aloud this prayer: "O Lord, give me the habit of continual awareness of Your armies surrounding and protecting me, and may I enjoy that protection."

4.   Write to Him your own decision, whether first time or reaffirmed, to give to Him regularly, generously (tell Him, if possible, a minimum of how many dollars every week you will give Him—1 Cor. 16:1–2), to turn your back on the possessiveness of your own ego and of this world.

5.   Release to Him, on paper, everything else you have tended to "own": people, your reputation, your gifts— everything to which you've attached the pronoun *my*. Give them, one by one, to Him.

6.   Write your own concluding prayer, worshiping Him in this surrender of all and in your enjoyment of moving into the valuable, the real.

If you're studying this book in a small group, read in unison together the prayer in the first paragraph above.

Read Hebrews 1:14 and pray the prayer in unison.

Read 2 Kings 6:15–17 and pray the prayer in unison.

In silence, individually write to God about your decision to give and release to Him the things you tend to "own."

Share with the group as much as God directs you about the prayers that you wrote, and close with prayers together of surrender and worship and joy.

Chapter 13

—of fearlessness and calm.

13

You'll have trouble believing this next story, but it's true. For many years my father was a general in the U.S. Army. He wasn't the typical image of an army general. He was a "velvet-covered brick"—strong and decisive, but so warm and gracious and encouraging in the process that he came across as if his greatest pleasure was to help his subordinates do their jobs well. Every command he had, officers asked to serve under him.

At the age of eighty-one, Daddy lay in a hospital, dying of stomach cancer. He was weak and thin and in terrible pain, near the end of his long struggle. Then a nurse across the room dropped something. Daddy sprang out of bed and retrieved it for her!

He didn't really mean to do it; he was embarrassed by it and probably exhausted by it. What he did was simply reflex action, the habit of so many years.

Well, "abiding in Christ" can be pictured a lot of ways, but think about the image of my dear Daddy in his hospital bed trying to help a nurse far more capable than he. The point is, abide in Christ and *stay there*. For your own good, rest in Him and let Him do His work. He doesn't expect you to do it for Him, and you can't, anyway. You're too weak to do the kind of business that only God can do.

Ego can get us in the habit of feeling accountable for all the ills of the world! We can try to carry a load that only God can bear—to feel guilty over all the pain and injustices on our planet, to groan under the weight and to think it all wouldn't happen if only we would "do" something.

The late Pope John was once begged by a very concerned cardinal to relieve the ills of the world. The story has it that Pope John put his arm around the cardinal and said he'd been helped recently by a dream he'd had. He said in his dream an angel came into the papal bedroom and said, "Hey, there, Johnny boy, don't take yourself so seriously."

Understand God's side, understand our side! His side is to let sin play itself out to the end of its rope and then to come in mighty judgment and set the world right. Our side is to pray, to give, to serve and help to the uttermost as He guides us—but still to hug to our hearts the secret knowledge of the sovereignty of God. He is at work. He knows. In the big picture, all is well. We trust Him. We rest in Him.

J. I. Packer speaks of "the gaiety, the goodness, the unfetteredness of spirit which are the marks of those who know God."[1] That's not a self-centered withdrawal from the world's pain; that's *knowing God!* Understanding the end and purpose of history frees you to reach out and help—in His name.

And in the meantime—the first page of my notebook always carries this paraphrase of Psalm 90:14: "He fills us each morning with his constant love, that we may sing and be glad all our life"!

Remember I told you that George Mueller used to say, "It is my first business every morning to make sure that my heart is happy in God."

This is characteristic of the iron only as it stays in the fire, not otherwise. There you develop a relief, a lightheartedness, an exhilarating joy and fun that knows God is truly God!

Ray and I were the speakers on a Caribbean cruise a while back, and on the cruise one day we ran into a lanky black crew member ankling down one of the ship's corridors, snapping his head back and waggling his elbows. "You gotta loose up!" he was chortling, "loose up!"

Hey, he was *right!* Resting in Christ *doctrinally* should "loose us up" *emotionally.* We won't be so tense! We won't get hurt so often. We'll laugh more.

Resting in Christ should "loose us up" *intellectually.* We can stretch to be less dogmatic on the fine points. Much as I hate to admit it, I'm probably not right nearly as often as

---

1. *Knowing God* (Downers Grove, IL: Inter-Varsity, 1973), 21.

I think I am! If we're rigid in our pet opinions, we're probably rigid in our muscles, too.

And speaking of that, resting in Christ should "loose us up" *physically*. We get so bloomin' serious over our foods and fear of foods, our exercises and fear of exercises, our medicines and fear of medicines, our sicknesses and fear of sicknesses.

Resting in Christ should "loose us up" *relationally*. We can be free to be ourselves and allow others the same privilege, receiving them as Christ receives us (Rom. 15:7).

And resting in Christ should "loose us up" *spiritually*. We may discover that what we thought was zeal for God was actually just a self-destructive intense personality.

—Yes, of course we should "burn out for God"; I want to, too—to live all my life for Him. But we don't need to burn out for Him like gasoline—explosively, burning everybody around us in the process. We can burn out like charcoal—slowly, steadily, over a long period of time, and good to the last golden marshmallow!

Rest, my friend. "Make every effort to enter that rest" (Heb. 4:11). *Loose up*.

Right now, relax. *Loose up*.

Be humble, don't argue, be teachable. *Loose up*.

Smile. Look up. *Loose up*.

It's God's way. There are troubles and pressures all around. But discipline your heart to *loose up*.

Are you exhausted? Your first need isn't a vacation; you'd come back from that and just get tired again. Your first need is to move into that position of trusting and resting in Christ—to *loose up*.

Are you in a deadlock with a teenage child, at an impasse with a friend or an employee? Your first need is not to kick them out, turn them off, fire them. First run to God. He'll *"loose you up."*

"[The Lord] will keep in perfect peace him whose mind is steadfast, because he trusts in [him]" (Isa. 26:3). He will not only give you solutions; He will give you settledness in the process.

Friend, *it's not your circumstances that shape you*. They are outside you and beyond you; they can't really touch you.

It's how you *react to your circumstances*. That's between your ears, and that affects the "real you."

And what controls your reactions? Abiding in Christ (John 15:4–10, KJV). Staying there. "Loosing up."

Then what if you find, for instance, a lump in your breast? Of course you'll make a doctor's appointment immediately—but that's external. What happens within? *Lord, nothing important has changed. You love me. Your eternal, perfect plans for me are continuing on schedule. I will praise You; I will worship You. I will rest in all You're continuing to do in my life.*

Or what if you lose your job? You'll be your vigorous, efficient self in looking for another—if, indeed, He wants you to have another. But all that's external. What happens within? *The Lord is my Shepherd; I shall not want. I will fear no evil, for You are with me. My cup overflows. I praise You for this opportunity to praise You!*

Or what if you're confronted with any trauma at all? Psalm 112 is a wonderful psalm describing the godly person, and it says "He will have no fear of bad news; his heart is steadfast, trusting in the Lord. His heart is secure, he will have no fear" (vv. 7–8). God's Word is God's Word! He's practical; He's realistic; He gives you every expectation of living on an even keel.

I've been growing in this—lagging behind Ray, but growing. Several years ago we acted with our hearts instead of praying first, and we cosigned for a loan for a dear friend. (We knew perfectly well Proverbs 6:1–5 says never to do that, but we acted impulsively.) When the fellow went bankrupt, the bank came after us and really cleaned us out. For a few months we expected to lose our home, our only real material asset. But God held our minds in the palm of His hand, and we were able to say, "We deserve whatever He does; we got into this scrape all by ourselves. But what if we live the rest of our life in a rented apartment? We still have the Lord. If we're really cleaned out, still all is well. Praise Him."

Grey Christians live from Monday to Saturday as though there were no God at all. They live as practical atheists, so they never "loose up." They fear sickness. They fear death.

They fear what will happen to their children. They fear losing their money. They fear moral breakdowns. They fear failure. They fear being inadequate. They fear others' thinking they're inadequate! They fear unhealthfulness in their food. They fear burglars and murderers and "ghoulies and ghosties and long-leggety beasties and things that go bump in the night"!

God doesn't want you that way. *He wants you unflappable.* Don't "become easily unsettled or alarmed," He says (2 Thess. 2:2).

In his devotional classic, *My Utmost for His Highest*, Oswald Chambers writes about what it means to abide in Jesus:

> God means us to live a full-orbed [inner] life in Christ Jesus, but there are times when that life is attacked from the outside, and we tumble into a way of introspection which we thought had gone. . . . Self-consciousness is not sin; it may be produced by a nervous temperament or by a sudden dumping down into new circumstances. It is never God's will that we should be anything less than absolutely complete in Him. Anything that disturbs rest in Him should be cured at once, and it is not cured by being ignored, but by coming to Jesus Christ. . . .
>
> Never allow the dividing up of your life in Christ to remain without facing it. Beware of leakage, of the dividing up of your life by the influence of friends or of circumstances; beware of anything that is going to split up your oneness with Him and make you see yourself separately. Nothing is so important as to keep right spiritually. The great solution is the simple one—"Come to Me." . . .
>
> Whenever anything begins to disintegrate your life with Jesus Christ, turn to Him at once and ask Him to establish rest. . . .
>
> Take every element of disintegration as something to wrestle against, and not to [allow]. Say—Lord, prove Thy consciousness in me, and self-consciousness will go and He will be all in all.[2]

_____

2. (New York: Dodd, Mead, 1953), Aug. 19.

In another place Chambers writes,

> Think of the things that take you out of abiding in
> Christ. —Yes, Lord, just a minute, I have got this to do; yes,
> I will abide when once this is finished; when this week is
> over. . . .
> Begin to abide *now*. In the initial stages it is a continual
> effort until it becomes so much the law of life that you abide
> in Him unconsciously. Determine to abide in Jesus
> wherever you are placed.[3]

Remember, *your real living is between your ears!*
Then make a constant prayer-wall around you that dis-
tances you from all outer circumstances, while within it you
rest in the love of God. You're at peace with His work;
you rejoice in Him. Let there be encircling you that shield of
continual trust in His continual work.
"Surely I will be with you always," He says (Matt. 28:20):

> The Lord delights in those who fear him,
>   who put their hope in his unfailing love (Ps. 147:11).

"But," you say, "shouldn't I at least have one fear—
shouldn't I fear Satan? Shouldn't I fear what he could do in
my life?"
What should be your attitude, as God's child, toward that
terrible enemy, Satan? The classic passage given us in
Scripture on how to handle him is Ephesians 6:10–18, and it
says that your defense is simply to put on the armor God
gives you and then to stand:

> Therefore put on the full armor of God, so that when the
> day of evil comes, you may be able to stand your ground,
> and after you have done everything, to stand (v. 13).

And what is the armor? Truth, righteousness, readiness
with the Gospel, faith, salvation, the Word of God, and
prayer (vv. 14–18)—all aggressively positive and happy!

3. Ibid., June 14.

Little sheep certainly do need a healthy fear of wolves. But if their egos lead them to think their safety depends on their own powers of confrontation, they could get *too* fearful and too "wolf-occupied." The most important thing their fear of wolves should do for them is make them stay close to their strong shepherd!

As we take up truth, righteousness, God's Word, prayer, and so on, we *are* close; we're within God's prescribed circle of protection. And we've become identified with all power and authority, so that in Christ our victory over the devil is already assumed.

> The Prince of Darkness grim,
> We tremble not for him;
> His rage we can endure,
> For lo! his doom is sure;
> One little word shall fell him.[4]

Then "cast all your anxiety on [the Lord] because he cares for you" (1 Pet. 5:7). He takes the responsibility. You can "loose up"!

Note that word *all* in the verse I just quoted. Sometimes we can get hung up on just one problem.

I know a pastor's wife who functioned beautifully through the years until her daughter became a rebel and married poorly. Then this woman took this care upon herself. And she went into such grieving that for the rest of her life she was disconsolate. She was a poor wife, a burden to her friends, a discredit to God. Her entire mental focus was on the disgrace of her daughter.

Cast on Him *all* your anxieties—every one. And if they come back into your mind? Cast them on Him again, and keep casting them on Him as often as you need to. Tell Him, "Lord, I can't carry this burden. You carry it for me. And let's make a deal: I'll take Your peace instead!" (see John 14:27).

But then, what if the thing you fear the very most of all happens to you? What if the most terrible possible

---

4. Martin Luther (1483–1546), "A Mighty Fortress Is Our God," tr. Frederick H. Hedge.

thing happens? What if God does to you what He did to Shadrach, Meshach, and Abednego—throws you into a fiery furnace?

The basic truth is that God is good, and he loves you to the end, and your reasonable expectation is that He'll give you what you hope for in your life. But *even if He does not*" (Dan. 3:18)—He is still good, and He is still in charge. He will still take care of you. You can even experience a holy, happy carelessness! You can "loose up"!

Is it a fiery furnace you're in—or is it indeed the fire of the Holy Spirit of Christ keeping you hot and glowing and purified?

Now Work into Your Life
What You've Been Reading.

1. Take inventory of the state of things between your ears. Are you aware of the "gaiety, the goodness, the unfetteredness of spirit which are the marks of those who know God"? Enjoy the measure that you do know God already and tell Him on paper how you anticipate reflecting that knowledge more and more.

2. List the bad situations in your life and, after recalling each one, write, "I flee to Your arms and rest there, my loving and caring Abba [Daddy]." Don't go on to the next situation until your heart is truly "loosed up," resting and praising Him in each one.

3. Memorize Psalm 119:14.

4. Put on the floor beside your bed a piece of paper that your feet will hit the first thing as you get up. On that paper write these words: "He fills us each morning with his constant love, that we may sing and be glad all our life" (Ps. 90:14).

If you are studying this book in a group, allow silence so group members can do numbers 1 and 2.

Then have a period of group prayer, sharing aloud with God and each other as much as He directs you to reveal of the business you've been transacting with Him.

Memorize together Psalm 119:14.

Number 4 will be "homework."

Chapter 14

—of restedness and strength.

14

For you to rest—that is, to live in total acceptance of God's way—demands quiet.

I don't mean a "quiet *time*," a period for Bible study and prayer, preceded by and followed by the old frantic rat race. Doing that gives your brain mixed signals; it breeds confusion; it gives you a grey life.

Resting demands quiet *all the time*. However active your external life may be, He wants you to develop between your two ears, in the discipline of your heart, a lifelong attitude of rest in Him.

To rest in God permanently means to hand over each activity, each situation of your life, to Him and to learn the habit of trusting Him to *work for you*.

We don't naturally rest. Naturally we are stewers, tinkers, and fussers.

I asked you on the first page of this book, "Have you too much to do?" Could it be because you're stewing, tinkering, fussing? Or are you taking on yourself what God didn't intend for you?

I know I'm rubbing the cat's fur the wrong way! Christians have copied the world's hunger to go faster and do more, to achieve and to be applauded. The only difference may be that when a worldling says "I'm beat," he'll head for a massage or a psychiatrist, but the Christian may try to keep going, keep smiling, and keep saying "Praise the Lord!"

Have you too much to do? Are you pushed, rushed, harried?

Said George Fox long ago, "Come out of the bustlings, you that are bustling."

To guard your inner life, you must guard your outer life. How's your pace? Are you too busy? Is your lifestyle allowing you only enough time to race through this book, or does it also give you time to react to it?

Does your pace allow you to *keep in touch with yourself*— with your inner needs and feelings and longings? Does it allow you time to think, plan, make changes? Does it allow you time to observe carefully the dear ones around you and care for their needs—physical and emotional? Do you have time to really *live*?

If not, do you have the courage to change? When you see the terrible pace and stress around you, could you dare to say no to it? Could you gear down to a different tempo? In the midst of all the craziness around you, could you live poised and serene?

Asian theologian Kosuke Koyama says that in human affairs God moves at something like three miles an hour, the pace at which a person walks, not runs! Are you synchronized to your world, maybe even to your Christian world, but out of sync with God?

You probably won't change just because you become aware of the terrible damage an overbusy life is doing to yourself, to your family, and to your relationship with God. Habit alone will keep the nervous St. Vitus' Dance going, driving you forward pell-mell—like a smoker who knows that every cigarette cuts fourteen minutes off his life but keeps reaching for another.

You will change when your inner life changes. But I just said your inner life is affected by your outer life! Then is the whole thing a vicious circle that can't be stopped?

No, the change begins with a decision. Your heart is your headquarters. Even as you read this chapter, make the decision, by a conscious act of your will, that you will learn to rest in God both in your inner life and your outer life. Once the decision is made—and you implement it as God opens your eyes to ways to implement it—gradually, gradually, over the weeks or years, the changes will come. Your heart will start listening to a different pulse deep within you, and with joy you'll begin to match your steps to that lovely, restful beat.

"Make it your ambition to lead a quiet life," says 1 Thessalonians 4:11. What a radical reversal of today's typical goals!

But you're hesitating about the decision. Why?

What's keeping you from "loosing up"? What's destructive in your life—what's driving you? Put your finger on it; it's not from God.

He says to you, "Do not let your hearts be troubled" (John 14:1). Don't allow it! Don't stand for it! "May the Lord of peace himself," writes Paul, "give you peace at all times and in every way" (2 Thess. 3:16).

What is it that's driving you?

Is it perfectionism? That's pure ego. You'll self-destruct! Confess your perfectionism to God and ask Him for deliverance.

Is it desire for excellence "for the sake of your witness"? Whose excellence, yours or God's?

Is it pure social pressure? Maybe you need to say no to some activities that "everybody"—even Christians—are involved in. They're sapping more energy from you—or more finances—than you can afford to lose.

Is it love of money? This is so serious it's frightening. Jesus says you cannot serve both God and money (Matt. 6:24); you must choose one or the other. Wrestle that one to the ground and have done with it forever!

Maybe you really do need to quit your job and rest in God to supply. Would you have to scale down your standard of living? Maybe so, maybe not. God knows the economic level best for you, and He's committed to supply that as you're obedient to Him.

Slowing down may mean a new style of living for your children. You lift from them the burden of "too much"—all the ballet lessons, swimming lessons, Cub Scout meetings, piano lessons, charm lessons, 4-H (all good, but too much). And you shelter them to make their own play, take naps, or just sit and dream.

You may need to lock up the television except for a few pre-chosen programs. Rediscover the "family devotions" of an earlier generation: regular Bible reading and memorization and prayer as a gathered family. Play table games together, or jacks or hopscotch. Get your aerobics jumping rope with your kids.

Or just sit! Be near. Be available when the questions and

decisions come. Be rested; don't let any seemingly good thing keep you from being rested.

It will take the discipline of your heart to shift down. For a while you'll feel restless, guilty that you're not "doing" something every minute. You'll want to "get busy," maintain the former pace, rectify every situation by your own nervous efforts. Who said it would be easy? *"Make every effort* to enter into that rest . . ." (Heb. 4:11).

But if you do learn to slow down, before long you'll know yourself better. You'll know the ones you live with better. And you'll have become a little island of poise in a mixed-up world. Your family, according to whatever measure of control and influence you still have, may become one less candidate for divorce, drugs, tragedy.

And you will say by your very lifestyle that you have time for life and for God—that He is the active One, working in you that which is well pleasing in His sight.

Now Work into Your Life
What You've Been Reading.

How easy it is to say, "Yes, yes, our society certainly needs this chapter. . . . My sister-in-law needs this. . . . My neighbor needs it. . . ."

Let me, Anne Ortlund, tell you, "*I* need it." In fact, God has just brought along a situation for me not to fuss over but to pray extra about. (Any tinkering on my part would needlessly bristle some personalities.) *I rest in You, Lord. Help me to learn the lessons I'm writing about!*

1. As you think about this chapter, if you know it, hum a little of "It's me, O Lord, standin' in the need of prayer"!

2. Make a list—written, or if you're in a group, verbal—of possible eliminations to make your home life more serene and oriented toward God.

3. If you're a parent, study Deuteronomy 6:4–7 and write in your notebook, or discuss with your group, how you're doing in that role. Set specific goals to help you shape a godly family life.

4. Write your prayer or pray as a group, asking God for the courage to "live godly in this present world," resisting the pressures of the age.

5. Praise and thank Him for His power to answer your prayers more than you could ask or imagine (Eph. 3:20–21)!

Chapter 15

—of your own uniqueness.

15

In this book so far, if you've not only read it but "done" it, you've taken three bold new steps:

1. You've accepted the fact that God plans for you a wonderful life.
2. You've admitted your own helplessness and sin, and you've determined to "abide" in Christ and His power for righteousness in your life.
3. You've faced the problem of today's frantic pace, and you've shifted down to allow that habit of "abiding" to take hold.

You've made three new steps to do two things: to get clean and to get rested.

Do you realize what you've done? You've left the defense and you've gained the offense in your life. Now let's go back to number 1 and see just what this wonderful life is that God has planned for you. Oh, my friend! You are just about to stumble on wonder after wonder, and every wonder will be true.

See, for instance, that God has made you a divine original, a one-of-a-kind miracle.

There are more than five billion people on this planet, and there's no one like you—nor has there ever been, nor will there ever be. Then dare to be His miracle! And enjoy it to the fullest!

God has made you uniquely wonderful, and living your life is a totally personal, between-your-ears miracle, shared by only you and Him. When you're sick, others can be with you, but they can't be sick with you. When you're depressed or when you're happy, no other person, no matter how close, can feel your feelings.

Except God. He has fused you to Himself (John 14:20),

and He eagerly planned that fusion even before the creation of the world (Eph. 1:4).

You are His precious, one-of-a-kind treasure. Do you really believe that? Said William Ellery Channing (1780–1842), "Every human is intended to have a character of his own; to be what no others are, and to do what no other can do."[1] From the very beginning, when you were only a much-loved concept in God's mind, you've been a combination of materials like nobody else.

Don't shrink from being what you are. Ethel Waters used to say, "God don't sponsor no flops!"

Accept your limitations light-heartedly. He made you exactly right. Are you below par in some way? Read Exodus 4:11 and John 9:1–3 and believe with joy.

Accept your strengths, too, with humility and gratitude. He knew what He was doing when He put you together. Assess yourself "with sober judgment, in accordance with the measure of faith God has given you" (Rom. 12:3).

Assess yourself honestly, and then—

Live in the sunshine! Abide in Him. Stay in your Lover's love (John 15:9) and don't wander out of it.

As you live there, my friend, you can learn gradually to be yourself, to become what God had in mind when He made you. This is so important that it takes skill, thought, and growth—to develop into being only who you are, your true self.

Baby Christians have to copy others, and that's all right. When Samuel was a little boy and heard God's voice for the first time, he had no idea how to answer. So he just copied what old Eli told him to say: "Speak, Lord, for your servant is listening" (1 Sam. 3:9). For his stage, that was fine.

But when Samuel grew up, he and God were deep, good friends and shared many joys and agonies and adventures together. Eli was no longer on the scene, but never mind, Samuel didn't need him to copy any more.

Grey Christians all their lives copy others. They're originals, too, of course, but they never realize it, and they don't mature into their uniqueness. They never grow up inside;

---

1. Laurence J. Peter, ed., *Peter's Quotations* (New York: Bantam, 1977), 374.

they have no deep individual roots, so they spend their life parroting Christian externals—the Christian words, phrases, and ideas that are currently "in." And they all sound bland and alike—their conversations, their teaching, their Christian songs—like pleasant tapes played over and over. They must be terribly boring to God! He hears the same few words and ideas repeated over and over around the world, as in a giant nursery school.

But you? Expect to graduate out of the baby stage. Look forward to moving beyond copying others to a wonderfully mature knowledge of God and His Word—and friendship with Him—that will bring you into your own focus and style.

Look forward to becoming *only what you are.* (Then you can really contribute to this world, because nobody else is what you are.) Begin to learn to "eliminate and concentrate"! Have you heard those two words before? You have if you read *Disciplines of the Beautiful Woman.*

Eliminating must be a very long, careful process, lest you eliminate both "bathwater" and "baby." Be careful what you're reacting against. Ask God for perspective; otherwise you could throw out important things—and throw out your graciousness and your tolerance as well. Use discretion and restraint in all your process of eliminating.

Nevertheless, as your eyes are fixed on Jesus Christ, you'll find yourself shedding what no longer represents you, what is inconsistent or superfluous. It will happen. Said Richard of St. Victor long ago, "The essence of purification is self-simplification."[2]

You'll find that you're deliberately unifying your life, your person, your style, your interests, your flavor, your thrust. God is one, and in Him you will discover more and more your own inner integration and coherence and order.

M. Dunnam wrote,

Isn't this our desire: to move through our days not as programmed and driven machines but as deciding, creating persons? Don't we want to be centers of spiritual power

---

2. Quoted in Underhill, *Mount of Purification,* 3.

and harmony, having at least hints of life infused with and empowered by a sense of the Divine Presence?[3]

Writes Meister Eckhart,

> All creatures struggle and strive by a natural impulse that they may be like God. . . . Whether you like it or not, whether you know it or not, nature in her inner-most recesses secretly seeks and aims at God.[4]

We have to admit it's true! God must have planted that within us. So when Dunnam asks, "Don't you want to be centers of spiritual power and harmony?" your answer and my answer is yes, yes!

And Eckhart pushes bravely even further into unexplored territory:

> When God makes man . . . He loves His work. . . .
> Now I will say what I have never said before: God savours Himself. In the sweet savour in which God savours Himself, He enjoys all creations, not as creatures, but as creatures in God.[5]

We tremble, we're awed. When we've fallen so far, can this still be true? Yes, the whole shout of the New Testament is that God in Christ has restored you to a far more exalted state than even Adam and Eve ever knew! It's true! It's true! God treasures you, He cherishes you, in Christ.

My friend, you're so forgiven, you're so perfectly cleansed because of the cross of Jesus Christ that you can really stand tall for all the universe to inspect. In Him—as you abide there—you are personally free to grow, to express your own will, to develop yourself.

Someone has said, "Love God and do as you please." And that's right, because when you truly love God *you please what He pleases*—and you and He are both thrilled.

---

3. Maxie Dunnam, *The Workbook on Spiritual Disciplines* (Nashville: Upper Room, 1984), 125.
4. *Meister Eckhart*, 179.
5. Ibid., 182–183.

Then live your inmost life in God. You are a twosome, and you and He can chart your course and make your agenda together.

Let every part of your life—your person, your style, your direction, your flavor—be in Him. When you're in Him, then you're based on truth. You'll be honest and genuine through and through; you'll be coordinated, all of a piece; you'll be in harmony with yourself. And then you can grow within yourself to unlimited dimensions—and all because you're in God.

Faddish lives age quickly. They're not based on God, who is greater than all culture and all generations, so twenty years from now they'll seem faded and "out of it." Anchor yourself to the great "I AM," and you will develop more and more into a woman who is ageless, whole, true, and at rest.

Goethe said, "The spirit tends to take to itself a body." And your inner life in God will shape the outer you in concrete ways. Only He knows what ways, but the result will be uniquely you from the toes up, whether you're presiding or helping or selling or studying or creating. It will be uniquely your style, built on your convictions. It will be your part of God and you!

And my friend, when you abide in Him, when you truly focus on Him until you specialize, then that kind of centeredness and concentration will cause something remarkable to emerge. In the "specializing" God will accent the "special"! You won't just be living in the sunshine, but you yourself will have taken on characteristics of the sun.

God will be developing in you the power to radiate and affect things and structures and people.

Truth is so powerful! Righteousness is so dynamic! Get on your face before Him and surrender yourself to Him, that this might be so.

If you're truly abiding in Him, *you'll affect things.* If you're artistically creative, putting together music or stitchery or buildings or lithography or poetry or cities or whatever, you'll depend less and less on copying what's already around you, and you'll draw more and more from the resources of the life of Christ deep within your own self. He is ultimate Truth, and you'll begin to reflect His integrity and wholeness in your own creations.

Ray and I must not write by copying other popular Christian books around us, saying what they say and hoping to sell as they sell! We'd be liars and phonies. We must write what comes deeply out of what God puts into us—what we've experienced and what we've learned. Whether our books sell or not, before God we must be true to our inner selves.

If you're abiding in Him, you'll also affect structures. If your job is to put together and manage people (you're a female office manager, factory foreman, politician, minister, company president), you won't outline your people in boxes and squares to look good in reports; you'll study their true situations, their work loads, their gifts, and their needs, and you'll work at building your people from the inside out. (As a mother, you'll do the same.) That's integrity. That's managing in truth.

If you're abiding in Him, you'll affect people. Jesus' last command was to disciple others (Matt. 28:18–20). And whether you're a butcher or a baker or a candlestick maker, you're to choose people to gather close to you, to teach and love and affect them for Him. (See my book *Discipling One Another.* [6])

To do this you must live in truth—sincere and genuine and transparent. An authentic Christian can say without embarrassment, as Paul did, "Join with others in following my example" (Phil. 3:17) and "I urge you to imitate me" (1 Cor. 4:16). But such a Christian is also willing, as Paul was, to expose his own failures as well as strengths. A Christian who walks in truth never hides his struggles on the way to holiness; discipling demands honesty. So Paul could say, "We speak before God with sincerity, like men sent from God" (2 Cor. 2:17)—like facets of truth sent from *the* Truth.

Now, becoming authentically you, a unique original, doesn't mean you'll say what no one ever said before or do what no one has ever done. It simply means you'll say

6. (Waco, TX: Word Books, 1979).

exactly what God tells you to say and you'll do what God tells you to do. Jesus explained it like this—and He's our beloved model: "The words I say to you are not just my own. Rather, it is the Father, living in me, who is doing his work" (John 14:10). Said Thomas Carlyle (1795–1881), "The merit of originality is not novelty; it is sincerity. The believing man is the original man."[7]

Then will you dare to be God's unique miracle? Will you assess honestly what God has made in making you—and then have the courage to love that and be that with all your might and no other? Will you fear only your sin, but fear nothing else?

My friend, dare to live fully in Him, with godly enthusiasm! (Franz Josef Haydn, the composer, was once asked why his church music was so cheerful, and he answered, "When I think of God, my heart is so full of joy, the notes dance and leap from my pen!")

Dare to enter into personal friendship with God as He waits for you to do. Dare to walk with Him and be absolutely free—in Him and with Him!

In yourself you're cold, black, hard, ugly iron—a worthless sinner. But in the fire you're hot and glowing and purified; in Christ you become "blameless and pure" (Phil. 2:15). One day soon the iron itself will be forever changed (1 John 3:2)—oh, praise the Lord!—but in the meantime . . .

Stay in Him! Live His plan for you with all your might! Be happy in Him; be happy in your life in Him; be happy in all He gives you and in all He takes away; be happy in what you do; be happy in what you can't do; be happy in all He makes you to be; be happy in what He never allows you to be. Be happy in you! Be happy in Him!

No more drifting, wandering, doubting, complaining, living in confusion.

Don't let anyone judge you (Col. 2:16).

Don't let anyone disqualify you (Col. 2:18).

Don't let anyone discourage you (2 Chron. 20:15).

Don't let anyone deter you (Mark 9:39a).

---

7. *Peter's Quotations,* 373.

Don't let anyone detract you from your goal (James 1:4).

God has made you alive with Christ (Col. 2:13), and you have been given fullness in Him (Col. 2:10). He is a shield around you, your Glorious One, Who lifts up your head (Ps. 3:3).

Then, from your stance in Christ, produce! Achieve! GOFORIT!

Perhaps you'll become so focused, so concentrated, that your sunbeam will narrow to a laser beam. People like this become the geniuses, the prophets, the ones with maximum intensity of power to affect.

Open yourself wide to whatever He desires.

Now Work into Your Life
What You've Been Reading.

This chapter takes time to digest, doesn't it? Read it over again, stopping at the points mentioned below to take it in for yourself.

1. On page 101, after rereading the paragraphs that say, "accept your limitations" and "accept your strengths," write a list of your strengths and another of your weaknesses (not your sins). Below the lists, write Him a prayer of thanksgiving for them all.

2. On page 102, after rereading the paragraph that says eliminating things from yourself or your life must be a long, careful process, make a list of what some of those might be. Hebrews 12:1 calls them "weights" or "hindrances"; they're not bad, they just don't reflect *you* any more.

3. As you finish reading the chapter, pray as Mary did, "Behold the handmaid of the Lord; be it unto me according to thy word" (Luke 1:38, KJV; Ps. 123:2).

If you're studying this chapter in a group, bring as homework what you wrote for these three sections, report on them or read them, and then pray for each other together. Perhaps you need to agree to check on each other periodically, to hold each other accountable for really eliminating "weights" and "hindrances," clutter and extras, from your lives.

Chapter 16

—of communion with God.

16

"Deep within your vast interior space," writes John White, "is a tabernacle God built to commune with you. From it He calls you with tender urgency."[1]

Have your inner chambers been unused and silent when they should be busy with God? Hannah wept over being barren: like a womb that's empty month after month, is your interior tabernacle empty—when God meant it to be a house of prayer?

Maybe that word *prayer* threw up a roadblock in your mind and you're back in your former rut of saying, "I'm so busy, I really don't have much time for prayer."

Listen, the issue of prayer really isn't prayer—it's God.

When Ray and I are in a crowded room, we may be doing different things and talking to different people, but we're more or less aware of each other. If one of us has an obvious need, it won't be long until the other has noticed and done something about it. And when other conversations end and other duties get finished, somehow, somehow, we find our way back to each other.

It isn't that we're trying so hard to stay in touch; eventually we'd be exhausted from the intensity of the effort. It's just that we're in love.

The command to "pray without ceasing" may seem like an impossible chore if you're "too busy" for even ten minutes a day. Hear it again: the issue of prayer isn't prayer—it's God. Prayer is simply the measuring device for the state of your relationship with Him.

If you're still a grey Christian, away from Him and living by your own energies, you're praying very little. And you're

---

1. *The Fight* (Downers Grove, IL: Inter-Varsity, 1976), 22.

"out of sync" with God's whole universe, and everything goes wrong. God isn't pleased with you; He rebukes you and hassles you and punishes you. He doesn't prosper your living; He doesn't honor you. He's a faithful Father who disciplines His children.

But if you have an honest desire to surrender everything to Him and abide in Him and let Him have His way with you—oh, my dear! You'll discover how wonderful He really is—how nice, how friendly, how eager to commune with you, how comforting and strengthening and delicious, how easy to live with!

When you look in the Bible at the people who set their hearts to follow hard after the Lord—see how the Lord actually winked at their faults and overlooked their failings! Besides, if you really desire God in your life, He desires it, too; He warms up to a person like you; you're what He's looking for! He will treat you well. He will bless you.

Well, then, that gives you confidence to start talking to Him, doesn't it?

And when you do, the blessed God of all grace meets you where you are, and moves you from there at the pace of your capacity, even at the pace of your choice.

> He tends his flock like a shepherd:
>   He gathers the lambs in his arms
> and carries them close to his heart;
>   he gently leads those that have young (Isa. 40:11).

Start talking to Him. Talk to Him right now. Tell Him you'd like to learn the art of communing and communicating with Him.

Wrote Madam Jeanne Guyon (1648–1717), who was often in prisons for her faith,

> Nothing is so easily obtained as the possession and enjoyment of God. He is more present to us than we are to ourselves. He is more desirous of giving Himself to us than we are to possess him.

Listen! You who think yourselves to be so dull and fit for

nothing! By prayer you may live on God Himself with less difficulty or interruption than you live in the vital air.[2]

Obeying something is always better than just reading about it. As you read this chapter, stay in constant touch with Him. Before another word, just breathe "Father. . . ." He loves it, and so do you. "The farthest reaches of your inner space," to quote White, are echoing back His call.

Something inside you is saying that this is more important to your well-being than aerobics or natural foods. Let this truth get a firm grasp of your heart.

Writes F. P. Harton,

> The Christian life is essentially God dwelling in us, and the fruit of that indwelling is the soul's participation in the divine life.[3]

How can it happen—that He lives in you and you respond by living in Him? At first, given the hard facts of living in this world, it seems about as practical and real as a trip to Mars. But—

> There is a way of ordering our mental life on more than one level at once. On one level we may be thinking, discussing, seeing, calculating, meeting all the demands of external affairs.
>
> But deep within, behind the scenes, at a profounder level, we may also be in prayer and adoration, song and worship, and a gentle receptiveness to divine breathings.[4]

If the world briefly calls for total concentration, so be it. But as surely as a freed homing pigeon turns home again, so before long your interior consciousness will begin to turn back to God. When you love Him, it happens without effort. It's what you most want. It's the least taxing and most

---

2. Sherwood E. Wirt, ed., *Spiritual Disciplines* (Westchester, IL: Crossway, 1983), 72.

3. *The Elements of the Spiritual Life* (Bungay, Suffolk, Great Britain: Richard Clay, 1933), 9–10.

4. Thomas Kelly, *A Testament of Devotion* (New York: Harper, 1941), 124.

pleasurable thing you can do. Says Frank Laubach, "To see anybody will be to pray! To hear anybody . . . will be to pray!"[5]

Listen, this isn't something you add to your already busy life. This is what you do while you do what you are doing! It won't take *more* of your time—it will take *all* of your time.

I'm aware of Him as I write this. I can't speak to Him in whole sentences, but I'm calling to Him to help with the words, and just now as I tore a sheet from my yellow pad I said, "I love You."

Be doing the same as you read. (What a mysterious link that gives you and me!) In between paragraphs, breathe "alleluia," or whatever comes to mind. Just as you breathe air with your lungs—automatically and almost unconsciously—breathe Him with your spirit. "Glory to You, Lord." You hardly knew you said it.

It may be a quick request shot up—a quick telegram, almost wordless, but you and God both understand it. Notice Nehemiah 2:4: "The king said to me, 'What is it you want?' Then I prayed to the God of heaven, and I answered the king. . . ."

Pray always (Luke 18:1). Pray continually (1 Thess. 5:17). Pray on all occasions (Eph. 6:18).

Where do you pray? In church (Ps. 111:1), in private (Matt. 6:6), in the open (on the beach, Acts 21:5; in a garden, Luke 22:41), on your bed (Ps. 149:5)—everywhere (1 Tim. 2:8)! "Pray in the Spirit on all occasions with all kinds of prayers and requests" (Eph. 6:18).

Prayer is for all the time. You pray when you iron, you pray when you jog, you pray when you take the train to work. But prayer is more than that, too.

A life of prayer is also a regular discipline. It includes a scheduled time when you lay aside everything else and give Him your undivided attention. Why do I say this? Because God gives us plenty of glimpses in His Book of the private lives of godly people, and this is what they did.

David was a busy king, but 2 Samuel 7:18 says that he

---

5. *Learning the Vocabulary of God* (Nashville: Upper Room, 1956), 33.

"went in and sat before the Lord." In Psalm 55:17 he said he prayed "evening, morning and noon."

The writer of Psalm 119 prayed seven times a day (v. 164), including midnight (v. 62).

Daniel prayed on his knees in his upstairs room three times every day (Dan. 6:10).

Isaac was praying in the evening when he first saw Rebekah and fell in love (Gen. 24:62–65).

Peter prayed at noon (Acts 10:9), and Peter and John went together to the temple to pray in the midafternoon (Acts 3:1).

Jesus prayed early in the morning (Mark 1:35), and even sometimes through the night (Luke 6:12). Luke 5:16 says that withdrawing to pray was His constant habit—and you notice He didn't just do it when there was a lull between events; He withdrew to pray in the thick of things and even when He could have been sleeping.

Scheduled withdrawing to God is what will establish, strengthen, settle you in the disciplines of your heart. Said Christ in John 15:7, "If you remain in me and my words remain in you"—that's Bible reading—"ask whatever you wish, and it will be given you"—that's a bold, free prayer life for total success. How can you turn down a deal like that?

And the Scripture must accompany your prayers. Oh, your need and mine is to know the Book!

Ray and I read through the Bible every year. This is our seventeenth year, and every year we see more of the Lord in His Word—more truths, more connections, more amazing structures. There is nothing like getting a sweeping, overall view of the whole, over and over and over.[6]

Stay in the Word even to catch the flavor of how to pray! There seems to be much prayer in our day with great authority but little humility. And yet godly ones in the Bible seemed to pray no "commanding" prayers; they never seemed to stridently confront situations, spirits, or powers. Indeed, Jude warns of "godless men" who have no awe of

---

6. Why don't you do what we do and subscribe to *Daily Walk*, P.O. Box 80587, Atlanta, GA 30366? It will guide you through in about twenty minutes a day.

celestial beings. And he points out that even the great archangel Michael never dared to rebuke the devil; he only prayed that the Lord would rebuke him (Jude 9). Sometimes I cringe when dear believers loudly, almost arrogantly, "claim" this or "pray against" that.

Stay immersed in the Scriptures to learn how to speak to the Holy One, your dear Abba Father:

1. Read out loud the prayers in God's Book, so that your own voice can climb inside the words (for instance, Dan. 9:4–19; 2 Sam. 7:18–29; 1 Sam. 2:1–10; 2 Chron. 6:14–42).
2. Put a Bible prayer in front of you, and use its form and general idea to shape your own prayer.
3. Study the postures of those who prayed in the Scriptures—and their emotions.

How should we pray? Seventeenth-century school children used to pray, "Grant that I may worship and pray unto Thee with as much reverence and godly fear, as if I saw the heavens open and all the angels that stand around Thy throne. Amen."[7]

Everybody's private living will work out prayer differently.

At this point in my life, I give Him the late morning. I don't eat until I have my time with Him, and I like that because the pangs of hunger prompt and accompany my desire to meet the Lord. I couldn't do that when I was feeding a family breakfast, but now I can wait, and for an hour or so I sit having brunch as I read and underline and take notes and write my prayers.

Then several years ago I thought about "the Lord's prayer" that Jesus taught us, and I realized I never used it unless I repeated it in a church service. And I thought, "If He suggested we use that prayer as a model, then I want to do that regularly."

So I do. As soon as I think of it in the morning, I start silently saying it—well, actually whispering, to concentrate. I may be out running or walking. I may be

---

7. William Law, *A Serious Call to a Devout and Holy Life* (Philadelphia: Westminster, 1948), XXV.

putting on my "face" before the mirror. (You may have trouble doing this if the house is full of kids!) I don't listen to any radio or television or make phone calls or get any outside input into my mind until I've spoken "the Lord's prayer" to Him.

It sounds different every day.

I may begin, "O my heavenly Father, more wonderful than any earthly daddy, may Your reputation be hallowed, respected, honored, revered—by me, and even by others through me." I chew over those ideas a while.

"May Your kingdom come soon. Lord, it will be wonderful! The lion will lie down with the lamb. Pollution will be conquered; nature will be balanced. People's creativity will be poured not into weapons but into peaceful pursuits—how fabulous. 'Even so, come, Lord Jesus.'"

Eventually I begin the next paragraph: "May Your perfect will be carried out everywhere in the universe, Lord—not spottily, in some places but not in others, as it is now. I pray that soon every created thing and being will be united in doing Your will; You deserve it. May every knee bow, and every tongue confess You."

Maybe by now I'm halfway around the park in my sweats; wherever I am, the conversation continues:

"Give Ray and me this day our daily bread—and how I thank You for Your faithful supply! Lord, give us wisdom for earning, for spending, for saving, and for giving." And so on, through the prayer.

Then I release my mind to the day's news or to other input, but I look forward in a few hours to a dead-boulevard-stop time to get alone with Him.

However you plan your daily walk with God, plan it! I give my next week's schedule to my small group each time we meet, so that it's there in black and white in advance for me to follow and for one of them to pray over. Then I'm held accountable for my life—for my walk with Him—the way I want to be.

Work to keep your quiet time enlivened and fresh! It will probably fall through the cracks if somebody isn't specifically praying for you about it and holding you accountable, and it will also fall through the cracks if you're not active when you have it! Write or sing or talk out loud or at least whisper.

Ray is as busy as I am, but his withdrawing time is just as urgent. Ray sings to the Lord every day; he keeps a few hymns of praise pasted in his notebook. And some of his notebook pages contain his prayer subjects: one page for each family member, one for our finances, another for Renewal Ministries. There's a page for his broadcasting on Haven of Rest, one for churches and fellow pastors he loves, one for the President and those in authority, and so on.

We pray together as well. In the car, going any distance, we pray conversationally back and forth. Every night in bed, last of all before sleep, we pray wrapped in each other's arms. (In Australia a fellow was shocked over that and asked if it was reverent. But we know our Father really enjoys it. We even thank Him and praise Him for our loving.)

Sometimes on Sundays I pray for all Christians around the world. I pray for those in the Orient who rise to worship Him first. Then I picture the wave of risers-and-worshipers as it moves westward with the morning sun. I particularly pray for our friends in Afghanistan, where we lived, who believe and therefore suffer. I pray for Israel, and for Christians in Communist countries and in Europe and Africa. I pray for the brothers and sisters in the Americas, who get up and praise Him last—except for the Pacific islanders, who rise and add the final amen!

> God Himself is with us.
>   Hear the harps resounding!
>   See the crowds the throne surrounding!
> "Holy, holy, holy"—
>   Hear the hymn ascending,
>   Angels, saints their voices blending!
> Bow Thine ear To us here;
>   Hear, O Christ, the praises
>   That Thy Church now raises.[8]

---

8. Gerhard Tersteegin (1697–1769).

What a lofty, all-encompassing business prayer is! We lift our hearts to God, and we discover we have joined a numberless company around the world and in heaven itself! We have left time and moved into eternity! We have, in a sense, shed our mortal bodies and moved, ahead of schedule, into our future glory with Him!

And, indeed, "prayer changes things." Wonder of wonders, it even changes the mind of Almighty God (Exod. 32:14; Jon. 3:10; Amos 7:2–6)! In prayer we have become "God's fellow workers" (1 Cor. 3:9)! We are no longer our little selves.

> Deep within your vast interior space . . . is a tabernacle God built to commune with you. From it He calls you with tender urgency. And from the farthest reaches of your inner space an ache of yearning echoes back His call.[9]

O come, let us worship and bow down.

---

9. John White, *The Fight* (Downers Grove, IL: Inter-Varsity, 1976), 22.

Now Work into Your Life
What You've Been Reading.

1. In your notebook write to Him your thoughts and hopes and longings of this very moment.

2. Then, according to your need, pray through one of the following psalms, changing the words where you like to make them your personal prayer to the Lord:

a. To worship Him—Psalm 145.

b. To admit your sin and be cleansed—Psalm 51.

c. To lay out before Him a problem—Psalm 20. (Add words to make it specific.)

d. Just to talk to Him—Psalm 25.

e. To rejoice in His safekeeping—Psalm 91.

f. To thank Him—Psalm 116.

If you're meeting in a small group, allow a time of silence for number 1. Then any of the psalms listed above can be prayed out loud, one verse for each person, still changing the words to pray according to your needs.

Perhaps you'll want to agree to pair off to hold each other accountable for daily quiet times, for as long as each person desires and until the habit is firmly established.

Chapter 17

---

*—of being equally at ease
with life and death.*

17

I was sitting in the back of the car listening to my two Ray Ortlunds talking together up front. The senior Ray, veteran of thirty-six years of ministry, was commenting on preaching to the junior Ray, fresh with his Ph.D. from the University of Aberdeen, Scotland, and just starting to pastor a church. Ray, Jr., is so smart (where did this kid come from?), and he feeds his people sermons from the Word of God that are thoughtful and finely honed.

"But remember," said father Ray to son Ray, "not many of your flock will ever be great biblical scholars. Teach them from the Bible mainly two things: how to live and how to die."

I sat there thinking, "My book is on how to live, but it needs a chapter on how to die. Both are so important for us all."

One of your heart's disciplines must be a complete, relaxed acceptance of your coming death. To dread death is both ignorant and un-Christian. In fact, one of the reasons Christ died was to "free those who all their lives were held in slavery by their fear of death" (Heb. 2:15).

(I had to take a break just now for an errand, and I was wandering through a department store. So many kinds of eye shadows, knee-highs, notepaper, strapless bras, candlesticks, clip-on earrings, fondue cookers, stereos, candies, fabric belts, machine-made Persians, overnighters, liquors, plastic cannisters, colored toothpicks—on and on and on and on. . . . "O God," I thought, "I'm on my way through all these trinkets to go write on death! How exciting! How eternally important and ennobling!")

Search your own heart. Do you fear the thought of dying? Let me give you three ways to break that chain and be freed.

1. *Call death by its right name.*

Death is death. You don't have to glamorize it the way some Eastern mystics do or dread it like the humanists. And don't get trapped into speaking of death in lovely but empty sentiments—"pleasant fancies of a half-held creed." Poor morticians—they have to think up every pink fuzzy phrase they can to substitute for the word *dead;* their clients might not be able to handle the plain reality.

2. *See death for what it is: both an enemy and a friend.*

Without Christ, it's the ultimate enemy. God told Adam that if he sinned he would die (Gen. 2:17), and he did—so he did! And ever since, sinners have had to concentrate on their sinful present because they're "deathly" afraid of their future: "'Let us eat and drink,' [they] say, 'for tomorrow we die!'" (Isa. 22:13).

A woman without Christ had better get whatever happiness she can scrounge from eye shadows, knee-highs, notepaper, and strapless bras—because death will be the end of all that and the end of everything in any way pleasant to her.

But for grey Christians to copy that—how terrible! For them to clutch at the trinkets of this world as if they were all there is—how unnecessary, and how tragic!

Now, we do have to say that death is also the Christian's enemy, in the sense that it tears us away from those people we love best. Ray and I often say it: "What would I do without you? How could I stand it?"—even though we know God's tender grace.

We've told the Lord we'd love to die together—if Jesus doesn't spare us that by coming first! But we know He gives "dying grace" only to the dying; we don't need it ahead of time. So we rest content in that and meanwhile hug to ourselves every day that we have together.

But still—I'm very curious about my own death, and very excited over it, and in a great sense eager for it; aren't you?

Dr. Carl Henry has written, "Death is a transition from life to life—that is, from creation life to resurrection life."[1] And of the two, which is better? Do you go up or down? We

---

1. "The Road to Eternity," *Christianity Today,* 17 July 1981, 32.

have a friend who chuckled, "If Christians had any idea how wonderful heaven is, we'd all commit suicide!"

"What a friend we have"—not only "in Jesus," but in death! Death is your dear friend who will bring you through the door and into His very arms.

Then you can keep light touch on your scheduling ("if it is the Lord's will"—James 4:13–15) and have a holy carelessness about death's interrupting it all.

One time, as a total surprise to Ray, he and I got whisked off by friends for a week in Hawaii. He thought those seven days were solidly filled with appointments and work. But I had secretly rescheduled everything and packed our bags, and before Ray could catch his breath we were suddenly transported to soft Hawaiian sunshine, strains of ukulele music, wonderful food, rest, and fun! Hey, heaven's going to be even better than that! And death is your transportation into the very arms of God.

One of my friends told me her little girl one day had a great insight. "Mamma," she said, "I know how Jesus gets people to heaven."

"How?" said her Mother.

"He kills 'em!"

How do you explain that one? Well, in a sense it's true, because "flesh and blood cannot inherit the kingdom of God, nor does the perishable inherit the imperishable" (1 Cor. 15:50).

Now, if Satan—poor loser that he is—gets in one final kick on his way out, never mind. Any sickness, weakness, pain, or even blood will be covered by God's kind hand.

And here's the point of it all: "Though worms destroy this body," said Job (now, there's your Grisly-Thought-for-the-Day), "yet in my flesh shall I see God." The end will be the beginning—glory, victory, and a bright and shining forever!

No wonder the woman of Proverbs 31 can "laugh at the days to come" (v. 25)!

> If we live, we live to the Lord; and if we die, we die to the Lord. So, whether we live or die, we belong to the Lord (Rom. 14:8).

3. *Learn how to live in constant readiness for death.*

This means, first of all, not concentrating mostly on your notebook or your wardrobe, but on the disciplines of your heart. That's the inner you—the part that's eternal, and you need to get yourself ready for your entire future.

> My flesh . . . may fail,
> but God is the strength of my heart
> . . . forever (Ps. 73:26).

You say you're only twenty-three and you can't relate to this? My brother Bobby barely had twenty-four years. My mother's sister had only two.

> Man's days are determined;
> [God has] decreed the number of his months
> and [has] set limits he cannot exceed (Job 14:5).

Our pioneer American forefathers slogged across valleys and mountains and open prairies until they came to a settling place, where they'd stake a claim. Then on the spot they usually put up some rude lean-to until they could build a snug little home out of sod or timber.

What if the wife had said, "Henry, I don't want to move! I don't care if you have built a better place; I just want to keep crawling into this little lean-to for the rest of my life"? Henry would rightly call her crazy.

So God describes our bodies as disposable tents, and he says that fortunately "we have a building from God, an eternal house in heaven, not built with human hands. Meanwhile we groan, longing to be clothed with our heavenly dwelling" (2 Cor. 5:1–2). My word, yes! Who wants girdles and permanents and aches and pains forever? And when God describes our future body to us He's limited to earth-words; it's the only language we know. But He means far, far more than what He says.

Therefore, my friend, detach your affections more and more from what you taste-touch-see. Don't detach your affections from the world itself—you're too needed (Phil. 1:21–26)—but detach yourself from a debilitating closeness to it.

Now, let's pursue this a little more: how can you prepare yourself for your own personal death, the only one you'll ever have?

By learning to experience solitude. By learning to enjoy being alone. It will get you ready for the ultimate "alone" experience of dying.

If you've clogged and saturated and stuffed your life with unceasing companionship, abundant advice—always the group, always the crowd—you won't know what it is to be an individual. And then if you're suddenly forced to walk single file when it's not familiar, it could be a panicky experience.

Get used to withdrawing. Get used to the sweet presence of Immanuel, who will never leave you nor forsake you.

Solitude is essential if your roots are to grow deep. "Each heart knows its own bitterness, and no one else can share its joy" (Prov. 14:10). "Know thyself"—which means, fortunately, not being an eccentric loner but getting very familiar with being a twosome with God.

Where can you go for solitude? "Jesus often withdrew to lonely places and prayed" (Luke 5:16). In a city, lonely places are hard to find. We live by the ocean, and Ray knows stretches of beach where few people go. There he talks to and listens to God.

Find a closet; find a spot behind your house; find a hiding place. Incessant sound will dull you, desensitize you. You were made for quiet. The silent forces are the great forces: sunbeams, gravity, dew. There is strength in aloneness, in listening, in observing, in prayer.

"Be still, and know that I am God," He says (Ps. 46:10). In your kind of world, full of noise pollution, *listen, in the discipline of your heart, to the still, small voice of God.*

Elijah stood at the mouth of a mountain cave, and along came a wind so violent it shattered rocks—

But the Lord was not in the wind. After the wind there was an earthquake, but the Lord was not in the earthquake. After the earthquake came a fire, but the Lord was not in the fire. And after the fire came a gentle whisper [a still, small voice]. When Elijah heard it, he pulled his cloak over his face (1 Kings 19:11–13).

Oh, the holiness of that moment! I think Elijah pulled his cloak across to humble himself, but also to shut out every other sound.

Some of our foremothers just threw their aprons up over their heads.

Tune out . . . and tune in.

Only those who live well, die well.

Now Work into Your Life
What You've Been Reading.

Ponder on your own, or discuss in your group together, how you will apply this chapter.

If you've prepared realistically for your own death, you have no assignment at all. If not, consider these possibilities:

1. Make a will.
2. Arrange for godparents to raise your children if needed.
3. Update your insurance program.
4. Consider assigning particularly treasured possessions to each of your children, buying a cemetery plot, or whatever appeals to you. Know that what happens to your remains is relatively unimportant and temporary, until Christ transforms it all in glory!

If you're in a group, discuss together an exchange of ideas on personal preparations. Follow with a time of prayer, thanking God for

—Believers gone on before,
—His promise of resurrection,
—Your own peace of heart.

Chapter 18

Move in beauty within yourself.

18

Well, you're coming to the end of this book.

If you read *Disciplines of the Beautiful Woman*, the companion book to this one, you were challenged to make whatever is your own private living space a place of beauty and organization and serenity.

You put a pretty basket for your makeup on your bathroom counter. You've allowed no more than a picture and a bud vase and a small book on the nightstand beside your bed. You're working at keeping clutter and confusion from the area intimately surrounding you.

But this time, reading this book, shrink the space even smaller—to within yourself. Dear feminine friend, if your environment is serene but your heart is not, you lose; isn't that true?

Right now, eliminate from mind even the closest circle surrounding you, and concentrate on your soul. Surrender to God. Relax; sink down into His terms. Let Him create in your spirit beauty and peace and rest.

> Hidden in the hollow
>   Of His blessed hand,
> Never foe can follow,
>   Never traitor stand;
>
> Not a surge of worry,
>   Not a shade of care,
> Not a blast of hurry
>   Touch the spirit there.

> Stayed upon Jehovah,
> Hearts are fully blest;
> Finding, as he promised,
> Perfect peace and rest.[1]

Now you may be joining Madam Jeanne Guyon and Mother Theresa and many others—women who through the centuries have lived in loveliness and peace and power without depending on any exterior at all. They've moved in beauty even in prisons and slums! Even if their most intimate surroundings have been beyond their control, in their hearts has been elegance and rest and God Himself.

Perhaps this book has found its way behind iron or bamboo or other curtains. You say you live in a totalitarian state and you have little or no freedom? Hear the good news: in the only area where it really matters, you can be totally free.

> And a light shined in the cell,
> And there was not any wall,
> And there was no dark at all,
> Only Thou, Immanuel.[2]

Or perhaps you say you're chained to an impossible husband. Think about Abigail: so was she. Nabal was rich but selfish and insensitive—a drunk and a bum, "surly and mean in his dealings" (1 Sam. 25:3).

And what was Abigail like? She was not just an escapist; she was realistic enough to call her husband a fool (v. 25). But she hadn't let him ruin her. When she talked to David, her speech revealed such a long-term inner nurturing of godliness that her words came out almost like poetry:

> The life of my master will be bound securely in the bundle of living by the Lord your God. But the lives of our

---

1. Frances R. Havergal (1836–1879), "Like a River Glorious."
2. Amy Carmichael, "Light in the Cell," in *Toward Jerusalem* (Fort Washington, PA: Christian Literature Crusade, 1936, 1977), 144. Copyright material used by permission of Christian Literature Crusade, Fort Washington, PA 19034.

enemies he will hurl away as from the pocket of a sling (1 Sam. 25:29).

Regardless of the crudeness around her, here was a woman of inner delicacy and sensitivity and beauty. Abigail's life was hidden in God. David recognized it immediately, and when God in His own time terminated Nabal's wretched life, David was quick to marry her. He knew a good thing when he saw it.

But Abigail didn't become lovely in the course of being David's wife; *she had already become lovely while she was the wife of Nabal.* Her real living was between her ears!

Or perhaps you say you're single and lonely: think about Ruth. She'd been widowed at an early age; she was childless; and she lived in a country far from her own home with a depressed mother-in-law (Ruth 1:20–21)!

But Ruth lived in God. Whatever her external situation, she was happy, helpful, modest, sweet—everything God wanted her to be. Her real living was in secret, and her Father who saw in secret rewarded her openly: He gave her a wonderful second husband and made her an ancestor of Jesus Christ (Matt. 1:5).

Or perhaps you say it's too late; you're getting old, and your whole life has been terrible: think about Miriam.

As a little girl, one of millions of captive Jews cruelly oppressed in Egypt, Miriam could remember when Pharaoh had ordered all male Hebrew babies to be drowned (Exod. 1:22)! So her parents had hidden her tiny brother, Moses, in a basket and made her responsible for protecting him. Unfortunately, Pharaoh's own daughter had discovered him and confiscated him and so permanently split up the family. And Miriam had lived all her life as part of a tormented captive people.

Then, when Miriam was in her upper eighties, something good finally happened to her! Was it too late to take advantage of it? Here were her two younger brothers, who had survived their ordeals but were now aged eighty-three and eighty, finally leading all the Hebrews out of the land.

Do you think Miriam complained about leaving her home

or about the length of the walk? Listen, as soon as the opportunity for leadership emerged, she was right there. And when everybody started singing the great song Moses had made up about their escape,

> Miriam . . . took a tambourine in her hand, and all the women followed her, with tambourines and dancing. Miriam sang to them:
>
> > "Sing to the Lord,
> >   for he is highly exalted.
> > The horse and its rider
> >   he has hurled into the sea" (Exod. 15:20, 21).

Her choice was in the disciplines of her heart: to be just one more little old woman in the world, or to rise to fulfill God's great plans for her life. She chose the latter, and for the next forty years she joined her two brothers in leadership!

Or perhaps you say your problem is different: you're raising your children in a godless community full of pressures toward immorality—so you have a right to stew, not for yourself but for your children.

Think about Mordecai—a man, it's true, but a substitute mother. Mordecai was one of thousands of captured Jews in Persia, where the culture was so pagan and oppressive that if the name *God* had appeared in the book of Esther that tells his story, the book wouldn't have survived for us to read.

Mordecai had assumed the responsibility for raising his little orphaned niece, Esther—and this in a situation where neither he nor she had any personal freedoms whatsoever. So when King Xerxes was looking for a new queen, neither of them could object when Esther was taken and put into the harem of girls being tried out for the king!

How would you feel?

Well, Mordecai had parented his little niece as best he could, and both of them were in the capable hands of Almighty God. So when Esther was away from Mordecai's influence and even in impossible circumstances, God gave her courage, and she saved her entire captive people from on-the-spot extermination.

How big is your God? Do you try to "manage" and "control" yourself and everybody around you? Is your mothering colored by every worry and fear, as you try to drive your children from behind?

Or do you lead them visibly from up front, modeling for them a life of rest and trust? Good leadership says, "Watch me. . . . Follow my lead. . . . Do exactly as I do" (Judg. 7:17)! Are you close enough, exposed enough to your children that your serenity and joy in Him can be caught? Do you "talk about [the Lord] when you sit at home and when you walk along the road, when you lie down and when you get up" (Deut. 6:7)? Are you abiding in Him as you live in the wonder of seeing Him work it all out eventually for good (Rom. 8:28)?

I'm in process in my life, too. The children are grown, and now Ray and I travel and speak full time for a living. And when I wake up in the morning, sometimes I have to think whether I'm in Cedar Rapids or Tokyo. We get jetted to time zones where our bodies rebel. We get put into very hot places and dirty places and cold ones; we can be paid well or not at all, given a luxurious bed or hard cots. . . . For a "nester" like me all this could be destabilizing— if circumstances controlled the inner me.

But I'm Noah in the ark! God has given me only one window, and it's overhead, so wherever I am, the view is the same. When I "blue sky," I'm being realistic—because my view is God!

> Be we in East or West, or North, or South,
> By wells of water, or in land of drouth,

3. Amy Carmichael, "We Conquer by His Song," in *Toward Jerusalem* (Fort Washington, PA: Christian Literature Crusade, 1936, 1977), 107. Copyright material used by permission of Christian Literature Crusade, Fort Washington, PA 19034.

Lo, Thou hast put a new song in our mouth,
Alleluia.[3]

Whatever is happening around you, first of all nurture
your hidden life. Become a beautiful woman—one whose
heart is nourished and lifted by daily Bible reading and
disciplined prayer. Luke says, "Be careful, or your hearts
will be weighed down" (21:34). Don't let it happen! Insist
on trusting Him! Insist on abiding in Him! Insist on enjoying
Him!

He will also be in you. Then, like a glove sheathing a
hand, you'll move only as He moves in you. He may move
you to be busy or slow-paced, but it will be right, and it will
carry out His majestic purposes.

There is no other way.

Settle your mind. Be steadfast in God. And there, inside
of you, He will create a heart of beauty and peace, rest and
hope, love and singing.

Alleluia! Alleluia! Alleluia!

And the direction of your life will not be from outside to
inside, so that after all your good resolves, people and circumstances will crush you and defeat you again.

No, "though he slay me, yet will I trust in him" (Job 13:15,
KJV)! And the direction of your life will be from
that inside of trust to the outside—to your family, your
friends, your church, your work, your neighborhood, your
city. . . .

Now hear a sentence from *Disciplines of the Beautiful
Woman* in a deeper context: "And from that well-tended,
precious center of you the circle will enlarge . . . and enlarge . . . and enlarge"![4]

My reader friend, were the proddings I felt about this
book right? Was it time for me to write it? Was it the time in
your life for you to read it?

I want you to know that I, too, am subject to its message. I
was fussing to Ray that I didn't have enough time to get it
finished by the deadline—and then my own book got to me.

---

4. Ortlund, *Disciplines of the Beautiful Woman*, 101.

I said to him, "Ortie, guess what; good news! You won't hear me fuss any more about that manuscript, because God's very words from my pen have rebuked me, and from now on I have peace in my heart that He'll give me whatever time I need to do it right."

My living, too, is between my ears.

So let's you and me, reader and writer, bow together before Him. He has worked on us both—in the reading, in the writing.

Lord, the two of us kneel at Your feet.

We live in a grey world—neither hot nor cold. We repudiate that. We vigorously turn from it. We spit it out of our mouths, as You do. We hate what You hate.

Lord, we are worse than we had realized.

Lord, You are more wonderful than we'd realized!

Lord, Your love for us, Your pardon of us, Your righteousness available to us are all greater than we knew.

Love so amazing, so divine
Demands my soul, my life, my all.

Now Work into Your Life
What You've Been Reading.

1. Write down what steps you're taking, in courage and obedience, to help you establish an inner life of rest and trust in God—steps to establish disciplines for your heart.

2. Share these steps with one meaningful person in your life—or share them in your group—so you can be held accountable and have prayer support.

3. Write and tell me about them. I'd love to hear. I'm praying.

Love,
Anne Ortlund
32 Whitewater Drive
Corona del Mar,
CA 92625 USA

CHRISTIAN HERALD
People Making A Difference

Christian Herald is a family of dedicated, Christ-centered ministries that reaches out to deprived children in need, and to homeless men who are lost in alcoholism and drug addiction. Christian Herald also offers the finest in family and evangelical literature through its book clubs and publishes a popular, dynamic magazine for today's Christians.

Our Ministries

Family Bookshelf and **Christian Bookshelf** provide a wide selection of inspirational reading and Christian literature written by best-selling authors. All books are recommended by an Advisory Board of distinguished writers and editors.

Christian Herald magazine is contemporary, a dynamic publication that addresses the vital concerns of today's Christian. Each monthly issue contains a sharing of true personal stories written by people who have found in Christ the strength to make a difference in the world around them.

Christian Herald Children. The door of God's grace opens wide to give impoverished youngsters a breath of fresh air, away from the evils of the streets. Every summer, hundreds of youngsters are welcomed at the Christian Herald Mont Lawn Camp located in the Poconos at Bushkill, Pennsylvania. Year-round assistance is also provided, including teen programs, tutoring in reading and writing, family counseling, career guidance and college scholarship programs.

The Bowery Mission. Located in New York City, the Bowery Mission offers hope and Gospel strength to the downtrodden and homeless. Here, the men of Skid Row are fed, clothed, ministered to. Many voluntarily enter a 6-month discipleship program of spiritual guidance, nutrition therapy and Bible study.

Our Father's House. Located in rural Pennsylvania, Our Father's House is a discipleship and job training center. Alcoholics and drug addicts are given an opportunity to recover, away from the temptations of city streets.

Christian Herald ministries, founded in 1878, are supported by the voluntary contributions of individuals and by legacies and bequests. Contributions are tax deductible. Checks should be made out to Christian Herald Children, The Bowery Mission, or to Christian Herald Association.

Administrative Office: 40 Overlook Drive, Chappaqua, New York 10514
Telephone: (914) 769-9000

 Fully-accredited Member
of the Evangelical Council
for Financial Accountability